Intensity

The (10ᵗʰ) Anniversary Anthology from WriteGirl

www.writegirl.org

A WriteGirl Publication

ALSO FROM WRITEGIRL PUBLICATIONS

Beyond Words: The Creative Voices of WriteGirl

Silhouette: Bold Lines & Voices from WriteGirl

Listen to Me: Shared Secrets from WriteGirl

Lines of Velocity: Words that Move from WriteGirl

Untangled: Stories & Poetry from the Women and Girls of WriteGirl

Nothing Held Back: Truth & Fiction from WriteGirl

Pieces of Me: The Voices of WriteGirl

Bold Ink: Collected Voices of Women and Girls

Threads

Pens on Fire: Creative Writing Experiments for Teens from WriteGirl (Curriculum Guide)

IN-SCHOOLS PROGRAM ANTHOLOGIES

So Much To Say: The Creative Voices of the WriteGirl In-Schools Program

Sound of My Voice: Bold Words from the WriteGirl In-Schools Program

This is Our Space: Bold Words from the WriteGirl In-Schools Program

Ocean of Words: Bold Voices from the WriteGirl In-Schools Program

Reflections: Creative Writing from Destiny Girls Academy

Afternoon Shine: Creative Writing from the Bold Ink Writers Program at the Marc & Eva Stern Math and Science School

Words That Echo: Creative Writing from Downey, Lawndale and Lynwood Cal-SAFE Schools

The Landscape Ahead: Creative Writing from New Village Charter High School

Sometimes, Just Sometimes: Creative Writing from La Vida West and Lynwood Cal-SAFE Programs

Everything About Her: Creative Writing from New Village High School

Visible Voices: Creative Writing from Destiny Girls Academy

Now That I Think About It: Creative Writing from Destiny Girls Academy

Look at Me Long Enough: Creative Writing from Destiny Girls Academy

ACCLAIM FOR WRITEGIRL PUBLICATIONS

Praise for *Intensity: The 10th Anniversary Anthology from WriteGirl*

"Many writers think, 'I can't,' or 'I'm not good at this,' or 'I don't know how to spell the words.' But the best way a writer can overcome self-doubt is to keep writing. These girls started with a few words and the seed of an idea. With WriteGirl's encouragement, each girl allowed the words to keep coming until her idea grew into an essay, a story, or a poem. What do writers do? They write. And how lucky we are to have these writers' words and ideas to inspire us!"
  – **Carole King, GRAMMY Award-winning singer and songwriter**

"The work of these young women reminds me what it's like to be young. Their voices are clear and passionate, carefully observant and exuberant. They celebrate their friends, their neighborhoods, new love, and mourn the losses from which their youth can't shield them. They tell the truth."
  – **Terry Wolverton, author, *Insurgent Muse: Life and Art at the Woman's Building***

"I have never owned a WriteGirl anthology that didn't eventually make the rounds of my friends. The writing is fine writing, and that the authors are young writers makes no difference. Art is art. Good writing is good writing. And every emotion finds genuine expression. Congratulations, again, to the staff, the volunteers and the writers who put great reading in our hands."
  – **Eloise Klein Healy, poet, *Building Some Changes, The Islands Project: Poems for Sappho***

"I expected this work to blow through me like a living, singing wind, having seen first-hand what goes on in WriteGirl workshops. What I didn't expect was the sophistication of these voices on the page. Poem after poem surprises me with its originality and vision; these are real poems, with as much art as street-smarts, as much love of language for its own sake as love of Krispy Kreme donuts, menudo and eye-shadow. It's a brilliant body of work. These young women could hold their heads high in any literary arena."
  – **Gail Wronsky, author of *So Quick Bright Things* and other books of poetry**

"These stories are immediate and engaging. The inspiration in the writing jumps off the page and wraps itself around your heart. WriteGirl does it again."
  – **Colleen Wainwright, communicatrix.com**

Praise for *Beyond Words: The Creative Voices of WriteGirl*

"There is nothing more powerful than thoughts and nothing more damaging than having no outlet for expressing those thoughts. *Beyond Words* is that outlet. For these young women, this anthology represents mental and emotion liberation via pens, pencils, and keyboard strokes."
  – **Felicia D. Henderson, television writer/Executive Producer, *Fringe, Gossip Girl***

"Powerful and strong, raw and vulnerable – these are the voices of girls who demand to be heard. Girls who know their words have real meaning, in a world that can often feel anything but real. WriteGirl's latest anthology, *Beyond Words*, is proof of their conviction. You will not only hear them, but you'll never forget them."

– Kami Garcia, *New York Times* **Bestselling Author of *Beautiful Creatures***

"Writing is the level playing field. No matter how rich or poor, tall or short, pretty or plain, if you can write, you can find personal fulfillment, build self-confidence and influence others to help your dreams become realities. Kudos to WriteGirl for providing young, female writers in our city the chance to learn the art of communication. The power of your program is evident on each and every page of your latest anthology, *Beyond Words*."

– Lynda Resnick, entrepreneur, author, *Rubies in the Orchard*

"Write what you know, write with passion. You won't find a greater group to offer that up than teen girls! If you want inspiring, gutsy, heartfelt stories, and you don't have access to a diary – here are voices, strong and passionate. Having been a part of a WriteGirl workshop, all I could think was, 'Why didn't I have this support when I was a teen?!' We all want to be heard. I love what these girls have done with this book."

– Rita Hsiao, screenwriter, *Toy Story 2, Mulan*

"Writing has been my life and I work very hard at it. Having a group like WriteGirl is an amazing help to those who love the craft. The mentoring of the young girls is a wonderful way to pair the professional with the new writers to show them how to hone their skills and have a successful career doing so. The excerpts written by these girls are inspiring and show genuine talent. I give a big thumbs up to WriteGirl and to those who are working hard to do what they love so much."

– Diane Warren, GRAMMY Award-winning songwriter, "Because You Loved Me"

"WriteGirl is a life-changing program that reaches out and supports young women to express themselves through writing. The dedicated mentors who do the hard work with them are guardian angels. And I suspect it is as life-changing for them as it is for the young authors."

– Naomi Foner, screenwriter, *Bee Season, Losing Isaiah, Running On Empty*

"Cheers to Keren Taylor for coming up with the dream of giving teenage girls a voice, and then creating an organization that made her dream a reality. Cheers also for her hardworking staff, and the dedicated volunteers and mentors of WriteGirl for enabling teenage girls to wrestle the truth of their lives, their hearts and souls, into literary form on the page. And another round of cheers for *Beyond Words*, the latest addition to WriteGirl's growing library of award winning anthologies."

– Barbara Abercrombie, writer, editor *Cherished: 21 Writers on Animals They've Loved and Lost* and UCLA Extension Creative Writing Instructor

"*Beyond Words* is an anthology alive with discovery, humor, and a keen examination of the world through the written word….It is truly delicious paging through this anthology, stumbling on lines such as these and those by 17-year-old Mikayla Cowley, "You know you're done with this world / When you're swimming into walls." This is exactly what WriteGirl is all about: removing walls so that girls like Mikayla can swim out to sea."

– Sholeh Wolpe, poet, *Rooftops of Tehran*

"The WriteGirls are woman warriors of the pen. To read their poems and stories is to be heartened by their wonderful, inspiring, regenerating powers."
– **Maxine Hong Kingston, author, *The Woman Warrior, The Fifth Book of Peace, I Love a Broad Margin to My Life***

Praise for *Silhouette: Bold Lines & Voices from WriteGirl*

"WriteGirl is essential to helping our young women know how important their thoughts and feelings, not just their looks and bodies, are. Right on, girls – WriteGirl!"
– **Nikki Giovanni, poet, *Bicycles: Love Poems, Blues: For All the Changes, Quilting the Black-Eyed Pea***

"WriteGirl is one of the most inspirational, innovative, charming projects gracing the contemporary literary scene. And *Silhouette* is one of its finer manifestations. These girls really CAN write!"
– **Carolyn See, author, *There Will Never Be Another You, Making a Literary Life***

"*Silhouette* is inspiring and WriteGirl is a great model for writers and teachers who are looking for ways to improve literacy and to help teens become successful through writing."
– **Elfrieda Abbe, publisher, *The Writer Magazine***

"So many know the woes of the writer. The struggle, the scraping by, the rejection. But beyond the mass of cigarette smoke and rejection letters exists a new start to a writing career. A clean one. A mentored one. An uplifting one. It's called WriteGirl...Until girls from around the country can access the beauty in one-on-one mentoring and a varied writing education, each anthology from WriteGirl offers a small taste of the experience."
– ***ForeWord Magazine* review**

"Read *Silhouette* and be dazzled and amazed by the searing insight of these teenage voices. Their passion and talent is extraordinary and uplifting."
– **Heather Hach, screenwriter, *Freaky Friday, Legally Blonde: The Musical***

"These are breathtaking works that explode with emotional daring, formal elegance and searing honesty. WriteGirl has unleashed a host of exciting new writing voices into our midst. Readers everywhere: take note!"
– **Marisa Silver, author, *Alone With You, Babe in Paradise, The God of War***

Praise for *Listen to Me: Shared Secrets from WriteGirl*

"The wit and wisdom found inside *Listen to Me* comes in whispers, shouts, giggles, cries, chortles, inner ahas, and other creative noises – proving once again that the voices of women and girls are as rich and varied as a great symphony. WriteGirl's newest anthology hits your funny bone in new places, strums your heart strings and strikes just the right chords to make your imagination sing. Listen to me, do yourself a favor and pay attention to what's being said in *Listen to Me*."
– **Jane Wagner, writer/producer/director, *The Incredible Shrinking Woman, The Search for Signs of Intelligent Life in the Universe***

"I love hearing the new voices in these pages. I've had the pleasure of being part of one of WriteGirl's workshops…Now when I meet a young woman in her teens who asks for advice on becoming a writer, I instantly say, "Have you heard of WriteGirl? Get involved with them immediately!"
– Robin Swicord, screenwriter, *The Curious Case of Benjamin Button, Memoirs of a Geisha;* Screenwriter/director, *The Jane Austen Book Club*

"WriteGirl is a dazzling chorus of smart, tough, inspired voices of independent-minded young women. Their mentors are professional writers who understand how important it is to let these voices be heard…WriteGirl is opening up a whole new connection to the imaginations of young women – and I say Brava!"
– Carol Muske-Dukes, poet, novelist and California Poet Laureate, *Channeling Mark Twain, Sparrow, Life After Death*

"*Listen to Me* is blood on paper, souls on the page. What courage these young writers have, what generosity. Once again, the girls and women of WriteGirl challenge us all to step into our voices with confidence and grace, and to sing."
– Sarah Fain, co-executive producer/writer, *Dollhouse, The Shield, Lie To Me*

Praise for *Lines of Velocity: Words That Move from WriteGirl*

"Unlike many such anthologies, this collection [*Lines of Velocity*] includes the work of experienced mentors…as well as the teen participants. The result is a dynamic exchange of shared prompts, ideas, and projects…The writing is at times hilarious…At other times, it is heartbreaking…This anthology is sure to be picked up by aspiring young writers as well as educators looking for inspired samples and interactive exercises."
– *School Library Journal* review

"*Lines of Velocity* is full of magic: Not just the wonder of raw, vivid writing, but also the alchemy of writers, leaping across age and cultural divides to inspire each other. The resulting work crackles with energy."
– Carol Flint, television writer/producer, *ER, The West Wing*

"*Lines of Velocity* sparks with the lively intelligence of gifted young writers well on their way to discovering the power of language. If I'd had the WriteGirl experience at the onset of my formative years, who knows? I might be a Pulitzer Prize winner by now."
– Suzanne Lummis, poet and teacher, *In Danger* (The California Poetry Series)

Praise for *Untangled: Stories & Poetry from the Women and Girls of WriteGirl*

"This fifth anthology…is a worthwhile and highly motivational compendium of poetry, short stories, nonfiction and dramatic excerpts from both students and teachers. Including great topic suggestions, writing experiments and insight into the creative process, this volume is a perfect fit for the high school classroom. Sharp observations abound…unconventional writing exercises… motivational quotes…nonstop inspiration."
– *Publishers Weekly* review

"*Untangled* gives me hope, riles me up, revs me up, makes me sad, makes me happy, makes me want to write, and makes me want to read. All I ever think about is how to make more young women want to share their voices with the world – and WriteGirl, plus this anthology – are actually doing it. There's nothing cooler than jumping into the worlds of these young women as well as the minds of the brilliant women who mentor them. *Untangled* rocks!"

– **Jill Soloway, television writer/producer, *United States of Tara*; author, *Tiny Ladies in Shiny Pants***

"This is the kind of book that makes you want to get up and shout about the power of writing and the power of women. It's impossible to ignore these teen writers, the pen-holders of a new generation of words, and their talented mentors."

– **Christina Kim, television writer, *Miami Medical, Ghost Whisperer, Lost***

"The writing here, always moving and sometimes painful, displays freshness, an exuberant inventiveness, and – surprisingly – a hard-won wisdom. Some of these young women will undoubtedly grow up to be poets, journalists and novelists. All of them have already learned to write honestly and with conviction."

– **Benjamin Schwarz, literary and national editor, *The Atlantic***

Praise for *Nothing Held Back: Truth & Fiction from WriteGirl*

"For these girls (and their mentors) writing is a lens, a filter, a way to cut through the nonsense and see the possibilities…[*Nothing Held Back*] suggests that reports of literacy's death have been greatly exaggerated, that language remains a transformative force."

– **David Ulin, book critic, *Los Angeles Times* Book Review**

Praise for *Pieces of Me: The Voices of WriteGirl*

"Wow! I couldn't stop reading this. Talk about goosebumps! This book will shock you – and make you think – and make you FEEL – all at the same time!"

– **R.L. Stine, author, *Goosebumps and Fear Street* series**

"All the boldness, unselfconsciousness, lack of vanity and beautiful raw talent that is usually tamped down by adulthood bursts from these pages and announces a formidable new crop of young writers."

– **Meghan Daum, author, *Life Would Be Beautiful If I Lived In That House and My Misspent Youth***

"*Pieces of Me* is a riveting collection of creative writing produced by girls and women with enormous talent. On every page you'll encounter fresh voices and vibrant poems and stories that pull you into these writers' worlds, into the energy of their lives."

– **Vendela Vida, author, *Away We Go, Let the Northern Lights Erase Your Name***

AWARDS FOR WRITEGIRL PUBLICATIONS

2011 Winner, International Book Awards, Anthologies, Non-Fiction: *Beyond Words*

2011 Winner, National Indie Excellence Awards, Anthologies: *Beyond Words*

2011 Finalist, Next Generation Indie Book Awards, Anthologies: *Beyond Words*

2011 Finalist, Independent Book Publisher Awards, Anthologies: *Beyond Words*

2010 Winner, London Book Festival, Anthologies: *Beyond Words*

2010 Winner, National Best Book Awards, USA Book News, Poetry: *Beyond Words*

2010 Finalist, *ForeWord Reviews*' Book of the Year Awards, Anthologies: *Beyond Words*

2010 Winner, New York Book Festival, Teenage: *Silhouette*

2010 Winner, International Book Awards, Anthologies-Nonfiction: *Silhouette*

2009 Winner, London Book Festival, Anthologies: *Silhouette*

2009 Winner, National Indie Excellence Awards, Anthologies: *Silhouette*

2009 Finalist, *ForeWord Reviews*' Book of the Year Awards, Anthologies: *Silhouette*

2009 Winner, Los Angeles Book Festival, Nonfiction: *Silhouette*

2009 Winner, National Best Book Awards, USA Book News, Anthologies: *Silhouette*

2009 Silver Medalist, Independent Publisher Book Awards: *Listen to Me*

2009 Winner, National Indie Excellence Awards, Anthologies: *Listen to Me*

2009 2nd Place, San Francisco Book Awards, Teenage: *Listen to Me*

2009 Runner Up, New York Book Festival, Teenage: *Listen to Me*

2008 Finalist, *ForeWord Reviews*' Book of the Year Awards, Anthologies: *Listen to Me*

2008 1st Place, Grand Prize Winner, Next Generation Indie Book Awards: *Lines of Velocity*

2008 Winner, London Book Festival, Teenage: *Lines of Velocity*

2008 Winner, National Best Book Awards, USA Book News, Anthologies: *Lines of Velocity*

2008 Silver Medalist, Independent Publisher Book Awards: *Lines of Velocity*

2008 Honorable Mention, NY Festival of Books Awards, Teenage: *Lines of Velocity*

2008 Honorable Mention, New England Books Festival, Anthologies: *Lines of Velocity*

2007 Finalist, *ForeWord Reviews*' Book of the Year Awards, Anthologies: *Lines of Velocity*

2007 Honorable Mention, London Book Festival, Anthologies: *Untangled*

2006 Winner, National Best Book Awards, USA Book News, Anthologies: *Untangled*

2006 Finalist, *ForeWord Reviews*' Book of the Year Awards, Anthologies: *Untangled*

2006 Winner, Anthologies, *Writers Notes* Magazine Book Award: *Nothing Held Back*

2006 Honorable Mention, Independent Publisher Book Awards, Anthologies: *Nothing Held Back*

2006 Finalist, Independent Publisher Book Awards, Anthologies: *Pieces of Me*

2003 Finalist, *ForeWord Reviews*' Book of the Year Awards, Anthologies: *Bold Ink*

Intensity: *The 10th Anniversary Anthology from WriteGirl*

Publisher & Editor:	Keren Taylor
Associate Editors:	Abby Anderson
	Cindy Collins
	Allison Deegan
	Rachel Fain
	Kirsten Giles
	Estella Gonzalez
	Rachel Hogue
	Anissa Johnson
	Reparata Mazzola
	Darby Price
	Glenda Richardson
	Katherine Thompson
	Jacqueline Wilson
Art Direction:	Keren Taylor
Cover Design:	Keren Taylor & Erin Fleiner
	Assemblage installation by Keren Taylor
Book Design:	Erin Fleiner
Photography:	Lisa Beebe, Clayton Goodfellow, Thomas Hargis, Mario de Lopez, Tiffany Peterson, Marvin Yan
Printing:	Ortiz Printing & Graphics, Inc.

FIRST EDITION
Printed in the United States of America

Orders, inquiries and correspondence:

WriteGirl Publications
Los Angeles, California
www.writegirl.org
(213) 253-2655

WriteGirl Publications
Los Angeles

Intensity

The 10th Anniversary
Anthology from WriteGirl

ACKNOWLEDGEMENTS

Thank you to the hundreds of women and girls who collaborated to create this book. We know the time, energy, emotion and perseverance you exerted to bring this book to fruition. Thank you.

To our book production staff and volunteers in particular, we are very grateful for your dedication. Through many evening and weekend meetings, transitioning from amenable to feisty to giddy, depending on what was needed (and what time of night it was!), you all worked together marvelously and contributed your best ideas and views to make this book shine.

Thank you to all of our amazing volunteers, parents, friends, partners and supporters for providing the foundation for making this book possible.

CONTENTS

1 I Am Complex (Identity)

Feel the Power (Los Angeles) 2

3   **A Particular Shade** (*Blue/Green*)

Behind the Glass (*Mystery*)   4

5   **Decisions, Decisions** (*Teen Life/Growing Up*)

10

It Swirls Around You (Relationships)

11

Crooked Jaw (Portraits)

12 Galaxy of Words *(Writing)*

13 Sing Your Word Song *(Writing Experiments)*

This is WriteGirl

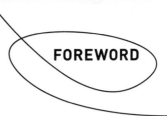

In writing YA literature, all we hear about is "voice." Voice is that one immense, invisible thing that sets a great book apart from a good one. You can't teach voice, and you can't fake it. You can only find it – and hopefully, free it.

WriteGirl is about voice. WriteGirl is about letting girls be heard (literally), about handing them a pen and paper (literally!), and about giving them the mic (literally!!) The two of us like nothing better than to come to a WriteGirl event, because it's where we hear real Young Adults doing what real Young Adults do best – if you let them. Being real, and using their voices.

This year, one particular WriteGirl afternoon stands out above the rest. It was open mic, and a steady stream of girls made their way up to "rant" onstage. A confident voice came booming over to where the visiting writers were sitting together at one table. "Girl," said the teen at the mic, referring to a popular YA author of a book we all knew, "You sure know how to write hot guys, but what is wrong with your self-esteem?" We all laughed, but inside, our voices weren't laughing. Could that same thing be said of us? Were we writing strong female characters? Was something wrong with our entire genre's self-esteem? How were we Writing Girls?

The girls at the open mic expect better. They've learned to expect it from themselves and their friends, from their teachers and their families and even the boys in their life. And if you're reading this – or if you're within hearing distance of the mic – they expect it from you, too. Their audience, their readers.

They expect better.

That is the lesson of WriteGirl. When a WriteGirl speaks, her voice is a powerful thing. She's not going to stop using it, not anytime soon. You'd be wise to listen. You'd be smart to expect something pretty special.

She is.

> – Margaret Stohl and Kami Garcia
> **Authors of *Beautiful Creatures*, *Beautiful Darkness* and *Beautiful Chaos***

INTRODUCTION

Reaching the ten-year mark is a significant milestone for WriteGirl. When I think of how far we've come, there are so many accomplishments that come to mind. Here are just ten that represent our journey:

- the thousands of girls and women who have participated;
- the hundreds of events we've produced and attended;
- the ten anthologies we have published;
- the 33 national and international book awards we've won;
- the dozens of bookstores and libraries that carry WriteGirl books;
- the hundreds of accomplished professionals and celebrity writers and actors who joined us and workshops and special events;
- the hundreds of foundations and corporations who have contributed;
- the thousands of individuals who have donated or bought books;
- the dozens of organizations and agencies we have partnered with; and
- the success of our sparkling WriteGirl alumnae, who are graduating college and embarking on diverse and exciting vocations all over the country and the world.

Looking at this list, it's impossible not to smile and feel great pride in our creative and community footprint.

Recently we asked some of our alums to tell us where they are and what they are doing. Here is a sampling of their responses – these ten young women represent just a fraction of the power of a decade of WriteGirl:

- Lovely is in Washington, D.C. working on nuclear nonproliferation policy and preparing for grad school in the fall;
- Anna, a recent member of the California bar, just tried her first case in federal court;
- Alma just completed her master's degree in urban education at Cal State Long Beach and is continuing her national advocacy for immigration reform;
- Lena is preparing for graduation from UC Berkeley;
- Jamillah just completed her first year at Dartmouth;
- Glenda is preparing for her upcoming year in Thailand as a Fulbright scholar;
- Ariel recently completed a journalism internship in Washington, D.C. and returns to finish at USC in the fall;
- Lia just finished her first year at Yale and will spend the summer learning Chinese in Beijing;

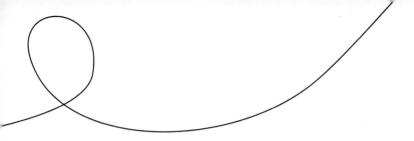

- Fahiya, a UC Irvine freshman, just finished her first film and will spend the summer taking a Spanish immersion course at Middlebury; and
- Mari graduated from Wesleyan and is completing her masters at the University of London.

These are bold, confident, creative young women, and we applaud and celebrate their accomplishments. I have no doubt that will continue to learn, grow and contribute so much as they make their way in the world.

But you are here, in this book, to enjoy the girls who are in WriteGirl now, sharing this space with the girls and women from our tenth anniversary season. These are girls who write about midnight conversations and running in the rain, who celebrate courageous women and are annoyed about alarms and excessive noise, who introduce you to characters with bad, foofy hair and lost luggage, who wonder about the content of their dreams and trapped memories, girls who are inspired by the streets of Los Angeles and all things blue. They share the space of this volume with the dedicated and inspiring mentors of WriteGirl, who have guided them on their journey.

There are ten accomplishments, ten fabulous alumnae, and many more than ten reasons to enjoy exploring *Intensity: The 10th Anniversary Anthology* from WriteGirl.

Personally, I will be using the creative writing, writing advice and the writing experiments within Intensity to unleash new innovative approaches, gain clarity of vision and boldly write WriteGirl into the next ten years.

– Keren Taylor
Publisher and Editor, *Intensity: The 10th Anniversary Anthology* from WriteGirl
WriteGirl Executive Director and Founder

(IDENTITY)

I

AM

COMPLEX

Write what you feel
and feel what you write.

Charice Barleta, age 18

I wrote this during a character development session.
This is about a girl trapped in her own mind.

Doppelganger

I am not she.
She lives in my subconscious,
wilting away from reality.

She is a step away from a deadly illusion,
always sleeping beside dreams.
She is the wide-eyed girl overflowing with life.

She jumps at opportunity,
even befriends fear.
But most of all, she is not me.

I am the pretentious doppelganger.

DeAndria Melissa Milligan, age 17

I chose to write this as a challenge. I wanted to write about an object that I see pretty much every day without saying exactly what it is until the end of the piece.

Colors

Sometimes I lay on so much
it looks like ink.
Its color is its trademark.
I don't care what people think.

Girls spend so much money
on so many colors.
So many options to choose from,
so many makers who are distinct.

There's orange, red,
yellow, green,
purple, blue,
and even pink.

But there are some girls
who don't go cuckoo,
don't go bananas,
and keep it cool.

They're simple like me.
I don't like it clear.
Oh, I like it dark and black.
Some girls may call that weird.

My reply to them is,
Girl, I love my black nails,
like you love
your seductive red.

Renae McCollum, age 17

The Perfect Woman

Look at her with realization
No hesitation, baby, see
I need you to grasp the meaning of a strong
Beautiful black woman
Your only opportunity to hold on to a woman
With goals and dreams

Fighting for independence
But still allowing a man in her presence
Absorb her natural beauty
See, I say absorb her natural beauty
Look past surface flaws
Appreciate the talented blossoming woman

She refuses to be held by fear
Determination, passion, desire, empowerment
Hug her curves
Hide in the sway of her hips
She is more than just her looks
Her mind should be part of your infatuation

See her, look at her
Appreciate your queen
The imperfect
Woman before you

Food can be inspiration. Eat.

Jia-Rui Cook, mentor

This is from a WriteGirl experiment where we wrote instructions on how to survive a challenging situation. I "recently" turned 30, so I decided to write about how to survive getting through this milestone with a bit of humor.

At This Point

Don't be alarmed if you see the simultaneous apparitions
  of three horizontal lines cutting across your forehead.
  You've now actually encountered things to worry about:
  paying rent on time, calling a tow truck for flat tires,
  choosing dinner over a buttery leather handbag.
  This will be the last time you forget your house keys.

Don't rush your morning. Savor that last sip of coffee
  with the newspaper, knowing the day doesn't start
  until you begin it. Put on the armor deliberately: beef up
  your eyelashes, check for stains on your blouse.
  That pimple on your forehead is merely a reminder
  you haven't outgrown all your youthful unpredictability.

Just accept that you're wearing loafers.
  Pointy-toed shoes with cigarette heels
  are for those who sit behind a desk all day.
  Besides, a new flock of pretty young things have alighted,
  and what's the point of being mistaken for one of them?
  Wipe the lunch crumbs away. Drive yourself home.

At least experience
comes with age. Realize you
are at a threshold. Brace your
hand against the lintel and
climb through.

Julie Aguilar, age 17

Being Latina

Tortillas fry
The scent lingers on your fingertips
Making stomachs rumble

When you dance
Square-waisted women watch you move
Aphrodite's hips entrancing

But some refuse
To let you glow in the darkness
You were forced into

Back straight, head held high
Many look down on you
But you bring their gaze up

They see independence
Intelligence
Resilience

You forgive
The world
It is taught to label

Jasmine Salvino, age 17

My mentor asked me to write about
leaving Los Angeles for college.

The Place I Knew

Little memories – pieces of what had been – find their way into my mind as
my life nears its next chapter. I remember going to the Bel-Air Hotel with
Halima at age seven, just to watch the swans and drink Shirley Temples. Or
walking to Roxbury Park with my parents, the smell of freshly cut grass filling
our nostrils. Or the trips home on the subway from Hollywood with my best
friends – our feet tired from walking, our cameras full of film screaming to be
developed, and our hands full of CD finds.

It is these small pieces that remind me of the extensive role my environment
has played in coloring my life – but then I turn to the details. My mom no
longer talks to Halima, who was a long-time family friend. My parents are no
longer together and we moved away from Roxbury Park years ago. Now
I realize that, in a sense, I am prepared for this huge leap I am about to take
by the innumerable life alterations I have encountered thus far.

Los Angeles will forever be the backdrop of my childhood and maturation
process, but this city does not define me. I am complex and life is complex.
I'm ready to set the stage for a new round of memories.

Always remember to write for yourself first. Your audience comes second.

Where I Come From

I am from chained men
Aspiration greater than pain
For whom giving up was not an option
I come from struggle

I am from the ashes and the dirt
Like Maya Angelou, still I rise
Like Martin Luther King, I still have room to dream
I come from wisdom

I am from flyers who soared through the sky
Like Bessie Coleman, first black female pilot
Like Marcelite Harris, first black female Air Force General
I come from courageous women

I am from tough times and standing strong
Like Nikki Giovanni's words,
"Cause I run the kitchen and I can stand the heat"
I come from strength

I am from a world that still has more to come
For my brothers and sisters
Together in the battle
I come from pride

Alice Cho, age 18

Time Without End

Without dreams, we are merely silhouettes
Ghosts lost in the darkness
Shadows of obscurity
Someday, our most beloved dreams will come true
And we will find the angel within

Hold these dreams
Pray to never let go
Embrace them, capture them
In the most cryptic areas of our souls
Even the pennant of death
Shall not taint the purity of our dreams

May showers of benevolence
Wash away the sorrows that bind us
With a seraph's augury
In time without end

On Fire

When I think of love
I feel on fire
When I think of hope
When I think of my future
When I remember the sky is not the limit
I feel on fire
On fire
I am
On fire
I must be
No one can put out my fire
It is my desire
That I am forever
Bright
On fire

Raegan Henderson, age 16

Where Is God?

Dear God,
Everywhere I go,
I see hate.
Are you all-powerful,
here to invoke love
among the human race?

I see unworthy death
and I have to wonder,
why do we love to hate?
Look away when we see murder?
Is there any humanity
in this world?

Why have you created
people who hate?
Why don't you save the innocent?
Where were you?
Where are you?
Will you be there?

Alicia Ruskin, mentor

*This came from a poetry exercise and the childhood
memory of a photo in National Geographic.*

Drift

my life is a translation
I seek truth
and find a thousand
the way it's believed the Inuit
have a thousand names for snow
because they are born to it

snow is the hard translation of water

in the packed and blinding fields
of endless snow banks, the head of a child
appears and disappears

we appear and disappear
following as chapters follow
a good read
I seek meaning
when I should be writing what I know

the taste of falling snow
the fleeting impression
of the next word

Kamrin Mara, age 14

I wrote this because I had a lot going on and I needed something to get through it.

Looking Forward

Looking forward towards the sun
Surveying the future
Regrets, none

Looking ahead and never behind
I run with the sun
My head held high

Beyond the problems of today
Moving on, clearing my mind
Can't dwell on yesterday

The hardest part is almost complete
Soon enough
I'll be back on my feet

Scared of the troubles tomorrow will bring
I know by the end
I'll want to sing

Looking forward towards the sun
Problems of mine
Handled and done

Toni Fields, mentor

I dedicate this piece to all the remarkable young women I have been privileged to meet thanks to WriteGirl. Pen in hand, we are free!

I Am

I am a piece of the sky,
a bright ray of sun
on a brilliant horizon.

I am a vibrant dark rose,
mysterious, but
always catching passing eyes.

Miraculous creation,
a thing of beauty;
never will you understand.

(Los Angeles)

If you're running short on inspiration, get out of the house and write about what you see.

Emma Holmes, age 18

This is from an experiment we did at the WriteGirl Fiction Workshop.
I tried focusing on a character's voice by using the first person perspective.

Asphalt, Los Angeles

A screech, a honk, and concrete falls towards my face. The 100-degree Los Angeles blacktop tears through my jeans and I skid, skinning my hands as I try to break my fall.

Like most things, I remember the beginning: my chest heavy, the sudden kick of vertigo propelling me forward. I remember the middle: the duck and roll, closing my eyes. I remember the end: getting back to my feet, the blood on my hands. It's the in-betweens that disappear.

Before I came to L.A., I used to live in South Carolina. Grandma would heat up biscuits and grits every morning for breakfast. She was solid – the queen bee of the hive. We survived off her willpower. Now I'm in L.A., trying to find myself, or whatever. It's hard being away from the hive.

I stand up, one leg at a time, and squint at the laughing sun. An ice cream truck heads around the corner, followed by half a dozen children. The old Mexican guy on 4th Street plays the accordion. A man pats my back and hands me a cigarette. Maybe Los Angeles isn't so bad after all.

I make my way back home, picking the asphalt out of my hands, a walking, breathing mosaic.

Kai McDaniel, age 14

My Home

I love that where I live isn't perfect – it's a lively urban city.

"Second largest city in the country," some might say.
I prefer "Home."

I can't help but sigh when the sky closes its brightest eye,
replacing the day with silvery night.
At night, everything grows.

I embrace her fully –
her imperfections, her sometimes pitiful clothing,
her vibrant personality,
her old soul.

I accept her for who and what she is –
Los Angeles.

Angelica Garcia, age 17

I wrote this piece about my hometown for a college application essay. I was inspired to describe a place that isn't particularly pretty as somewhere warm and wonderful.

Clark Avenue

The first place I lived was a masterpiece under a blanket of staccato Spanish, crying children, car alarms, gossiping old women and merengue music.

El Monte, just east of Los Angeles, is not beautiful in the conventional sense. Half of the people who live there don't take care of their lawns or pick up after the messes they make on the sidewalk. There is always some liquid trickling along the curbs. I see what makes the city ugly in the eyes of most passersby, but I also know there's a side of this city that's invisible to them.

My grandparents' street, Clark Avenue, stays the same. With each visit to their neighborhood, I'm greeted by music on the sidewalk. Sometimes the sound is coming from my grandparents' house. Sometimes it's coming from a neighbor's. Clark Avenue is also full of voices engaged in small conversations. On this street, everyone wants to be updated on each other's stories.

I feel like I am a granddaughter to at least three different *señoras*, the old women who wear muumuus with flowered patterns and exchange medical remedies and hearsay over their fences as they water thirsty gardens.

As I step inside my grandparents' house, I am greeted by the various saints hanging on the living room walls. Their holy faces are calm and thoughtful. They extend their arms as if they are granting me blessings. Now, more than ever, I appreciate the city, the neighborhood and this house, because I fear I'll run out of time to absorb them all.

Pick a random word, then write about it.

Shue-li Rozen, age 16

*Grass grows out of cracks and lines in concrete,
and I thought it would be interesting to write about it.
Then things took a strange turn.*

Green Enemy

In one swift motion, I bend down, tear the sprig from the ground and leave its roots without anything to hold. The meaningless green shoots fall into my black trash bag with all the others I have already destroyed. My toes curl in disgust as I stare down at another green sprig erupting from the gray sidewalk crack. This one is a little bigger, but nothing my pincers won't solve. I attack it like a knife hacking at a fresh cantaloupe.

We make Los Angeles beautiful, and it makes us feel empowered every night. Prowling about with LED flashlights around our heads, we scour the city for all the green that does not belong. We slip on oversized and weathered gloves that feel like furnaces inside and work until our hands have morphed into lava-hot claws that follow orders. It becomes a need for us; a need that penetrates and permeates deep into our souls. Green is our enemy, disrupting our shiny city, and we work hard to make sure that the battle we fight against it is won.

Ah! Another evil little sprig in the crack just a few steps away. It is a little bigger, I realize, as my shoes squeak and tap out a rhythm against the smooth concrete, but nothing my pincers won't solve.

Green is our enemy. Without it, our city will shine like the Hollywood stars.

Nicole Nitta, age 16

*As a lifelong resident of Los Angeles, I've realized how
much the environment helped make me who I am.
This is a personal reflection on the ups and downs of the city.*

An Extreme Personality

Seventeen years
of connecting with her
have produced
a love-hate relationship.

She's warm and sunny, full of life,
radiating a unique sense of style.
Full of ambition, she's a beacon of hope
for those who want to rediscover themselves.

A shining star on the Walk of Fame,
she's a model of the California dream.
But her glow, I've found,
can dissolve easily.

Nonstop energy
can be exhausting.
(She rarely
takes a break.)

Staying up late with her
can be a wild card,
sometimes dangerous,
and she's constantly stuck behind the wheel.

My entire life
has been shaped by her,
the city,
Los Angeles.

Sarah Huda, age 17

*I've been working on a novel with my mentor, Lisa.
The main character, Chuck, is a man who lost his memory.
In this section, Chuck and his friend Joseph visit
Chuck's office, searching for answers.*

Beneath the Smog (an excerpt)

Chuck and Joseph walked into the lobby and headed for the front desk. The receptionist, who had a huge smile and an annoying operator voice, typed and clicked away. They greeted her with "Good morning!"

She looked up and did a double take. "Good morning, Mr. Holmes! Have a nice vacation?"

"Umm…yeah." Chuck paused. "Where is my office again?"

"Well, I guess you were on vacation too long!" She began laughing hysterically as she slapped her thigh. "It's on the thirtieth floor, first door after the elevator opens. Or are you going to take the stairs so you can maintain those good looks?" She leaned over the tall desk and squeezed his arm muscle. He pulled back with a look of bewilderment.

"Thanks," he uttered as he jumped into the elevator.

The elevator opened, revealing large double doors with a golden plaque that read *Charles Holmes*. Chuck and Joseph walked into an office with ceiling-to-floor windows. They were taken aback by the view. There was a thin layer of smog that seemed to capture the true essence of L.A. Beneath the smog were bright, clear, powder-blue skies. They could see all of Los Angeles. Far to the left was the Hollywood sign, and straight ahead, the heart of downtown. The U.S. Bank building and the gorgeous new Ritz Carlton glimmered in the sun.

"It feels as if we are floating among the clouds," Joseph said. He sat in the chair behind the grandiose oak desk and spun around. Grabbing onto the table, he screamed, "I feel the power!"

Kamryn Barker, age 16

I was inspired by my memories of teen clubs and the local beaches.

My L.A.

I hit the club at night
head to the beach
by day

Dive into the sun
journey through the waves
sink into the sand

I escape my pain
all my troubles
and the rain

I get a hot dog
at the boardwalk
fill up with joy

Hang out
with friends
meet a couple of boys

It's just another
summer day
in my L.A.

Write from
your heart.
Your enthusiasm
will shine through.

Greer Silverman, age 17

This piece is inspired by Joan Didion. I wanted to capture the frustration and anger prevalent during the recent fires in Los Angeles.

My Los Angeles

It is August. The smoggy haze that hangs over the city has been suspended only to be replaced with a thicker curtain. The wind does not blow through the palms. The clouds have turned an ugly gray and there is ash on the car. I don't leave the house.

Overnight, the windows have transformed. The rusty latches are stiff and uncooperative. They are coated in a fine, powdery dusting, but it is August, and it is Los Angeles, and the flecks are too dirty to be snow. The panes creak open a crack, but there is no wind, no coolness, no motion. Heat filters in through the screen. The air is sickly and orange and hard to breathe – it works its way into my lungs. Shielding my mouth, I suck at the air between my fingers, but it still burns the same, ash still gets in, and now my throat tastes of it.

This is an August day that I will spend on the floor, in self-pity. Calls will go ignored and eventually the ringing will stop entirely. There will be slamming, of fists, of feet, of phones and of doors. Someone will get cursed out. My lips will crack. Old arguments will play themselves on repeat and I will spend all day re-fighting them.

Tourists will not see this California. For them, Los Angeles will always be a sort of paradise – strange and beyond their grasp, but still paradise. For them, Pompeii is a morbid historical story, not the fourth week of August and the first two of September. For them, the theoretical and the actual are two different places. At least they have never watched the world end and burn, and end again.

Calia Anderson, age 16

When I was younger, I always saw names scratched into the sidewalk down the street from my house. One night, I was walking with my mom and we started to talk about what the names meant and who they were.

125th Street

Sixteen colored boxes, old and faded, line a cracked street. Sixteen little worlds, each with its own story, full of people I know nothing about. Sixteen years I've lived here, but tonight a story appears. Thirty years ago, they carved their names into the sidewalk.

Charlene went into labor after being carjacked. And the others, the ones even my mom doesn't know? Pops, Theo and Alicia, Ms. Tee, and Mr. Pork – six people, a little pink box, and an old cracked street.

Who are these people who etched their names in the ground, forever leaving their mark on my block? Where are they now? Does this empty house hold their stories, or is the small patch of sidewalk just a distant memory?

Sarah Tuibeo, age 16

A Song for Los Angeles

Famous Hollywood sign
Beverly Hills, green light
In the dead night of Los Angeles

One more day and night
One more chance to fly
One more chance to die
My chance, my time, my chance tonight

Chorus:

The city of your dreams
The city where everything
Is not what it seems
This city's killing me
The city where legends live forever
City of "Fame Glamour Disorder"
Love and hate
Seize the city of Los Angeles

One more time, you call my name
I'll never ever be the same
It's my time to ignite the flame
In the heart of Los Angeles

Linda Folsom, mentor

My mentee Piers and I brainstormed ideas for writing about Los Angeles. We decided to use neighborhoods as metaphors.

Personal Geography

I used to be Venice
Wildness and adventure
Life was tangy, salty
Filled with sunshine and surf

I aspired to be Bel-Air
Fantasy behind gated driveways
Possibilities and promises
Just beyond reach

Then I was Westwood
Bookstores and cafes
Pretending erudition
Debating Descartes until midnight

Post-college I inhabited Hollywood
Shared apartments and rented homes
Freelance challenges, tasted temptation
Stood my ground

Then I became Mt. Washington
One thousand square feet of responsibility
Manicured lawns and motherhood
Babysitting, co-ops and carpools

Today I am 3,000 square feet
Of empty nest wondering
Will I be Silverlake or Burbank
San Diego or San Francisco

Will I be Maine, Oregon
Or Hawaii or all three
Wherever I am, I will be
California, full of dreams

Find inspiration in
a newspaper article.
Start your story
where the article ends.

Lyla Matar, age 13

This song is inspired by the city of Los Angeles and the feelings it conjures in me. It is also about how this city is like a mother to me and how it not only creates dreams, but characters, too.

Dreaming of a City

I dream of a city
The angels sing about
I dream of a city
That's hidden in the clouds

And she calls to me
She whispers my name
Behind all the makeup
She remains unchanged

I walk through the city
And watch the children play
Life blooms like flowers
As the sun shines down on me

And she calls to me
She whispers my name
And she is my mother
She helps guide me

And she is the city
That'll make your blood run cold
And she is the city
With a hatred so old

And she calls to me
To wash me clean
With bloodied hands
Wild and untamed
I dream of a city.

Laura Lujan, age 15

I woke up one day and my house was buzzing with noise.
It made me angry and I wished for silent mornings.
I decided to write a poem about the millions of sounds
that can happen in just one day.

In Just One Day

An alarm clock buzzes
My sister groans from across the room
Walls chiseled with our dreams
Footsteps stomp across the hardwood floor
A toilet flushes. A shower pounds
water down a drain
The toaster radiates heat, then,
Spring!

A car starts
Another shrieks, alarmed
A third beeps then zooms
Radios SCREAM
"Hello" "Hi" "Hey" "Hello" *"Buenos días"* "Hello"
Hugs and kisses
Laughing in the distance
A construction site nearby
POUND, POUND, POUNDING of steel

A dog barks, a cat hisses
A baby cries, a mother hushes
Glass falls – CRASH!

Overhead satellites beep
A plane engine roars
Trees rustle and talk
Anger leads to yells
Then silence in the night
But somewhere
An alarm clock buzzes

Guadalupe Mendoza, age 14

I was trying to get to a WriteGirl workshop on time but, as we all know, downtown L.A. during morning rush hour is not fun. My father suggested we take the side streets instead of the freeway.

Father Knows Best

Adversity was hidden
In every turn

We might not have noticed
Any other choice

It's time to do this
The old-fashioned way

Vasti Carrion, age 18

I wrote this piece about L.A. to express my desire to get out more into the city. I am at home a lot, so I want to get out on my own.

What This City Can Be

I hope to go
Around and about

I hope to see
Santa Monica, Long Beach

I hope to know
Downtown L.A.

I hope to go
Exploring up and down

I hope to see
Museums, Topanga Creek

I hope to know
What this city can be

Kirsten Giles, mentor

This piece came from a word challenge activity where I had a list of seven words (including Chautauqua) and had to write a poem that used them all.

Sunday Morning

I drive west on Sunset Boulevard
past those homes on stilts, precarious
treehouses of the rich and famous

Where Chautauqua descends
to the sparkling beachfront,
the sugar-sweet smell of honeysuckle
fills the air.

Surfers break the glass of the ocean,
start their optimistic paddling,
while seagulls shriek
like toddlers in the morning.

I dragged myself here
from a homebody moment,
from the shelter of an old Victorian,
to see this sunrise,

to restore my belief
in new beginnings,
and to dust the tops of my feet with sand.

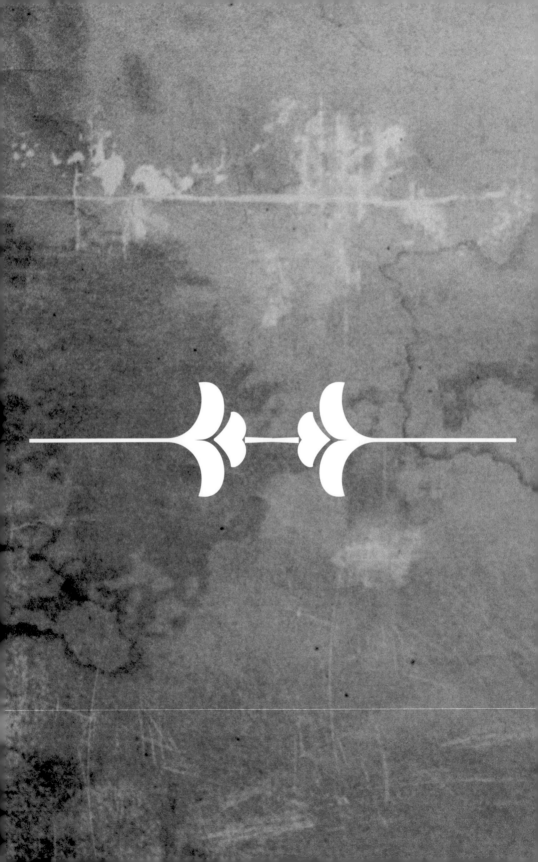

A PARTICULAR SHADE

Don't clutter.
Trim the excess.
Sculpt your work.
<u>Less is</u> more.

Isabella Lloyd-Damnjanovic, age 15

This piece was inspired by the idea of blue more as an
emotion and less as a color. It came partly from a dream.

Her Voice Is Blue

Louisiana blue,
bayou blue,
lonely,
fragile,
abandoned blue.

Silvery-gray blue, chalky Eucalyptus leaves in a trembling breeze.

Bubbles catch in her throat and erupt in little trills.
Her lips move and thin reedy Southern summer blues
chase each other down her hips and crest
like the foam of a breaking wave,

turn into broad brushstrokes,
soaking watercolors that swirl and pool at her feet.

Her eyelashes flutter and silver glitters of dark,
bruised blue, miles of velvet
bind to whispered words that shiver in the hush of a still June night.

Terrible, beautiful blue.

Molly Hennessy-Fiske, mentor

I learned about list poems at a WriteGirl workshop and love working on them with my mentee, Corine. I have also learned to channel my strongest emotions into poetry. When I saw a sign outside my door that irritated me, I stopped, examined the emotion, and tried to translate it into poetry.

Lemon Tree

Heart of February
Cold penetrates
My windows.
And yet,
Outside, the succulent tree
Still thrives, its
Child-size branches
Greening
Ever upward
Bursting towards
A golden harvest,
Stocked with
Promise.
Until the day
A sign sprouts:
"Please do not take lemons."
Oh, possession!
You bitter, bitter fruit.

I wanted to write a fiction piece after a WriteGirl workshop.
The words "blue" and "green" triggered an idea for
a short piece about a girl who wakes up as a lizard.

Iridescent

This morning, I woke up as a giant lizard.

It takes me a minute to figure it out: hot, reeking breath and a thick tongue clogging my mouth. Gross. My lips are laminate edges when I lick them. My bulging eyes careen on either side of my head. I can see my entire room without moving. Sweet!

The cotton flowers on the pillowcase fall into punctured shreds as I lunge myself up. My tail thunks across the nightstand, sweeping scented candles and books into a tumble on the floor. I waterfall my limbs and body onto forgiving plush.

Why does it take so long to cross my room? Sun rays sprinkle about my scales. I stop to watch the light show of jade, fern and turquoise…I am emerald, indigo and kelly shades of cool. I am gorgeous!

Languidly swaying into my little brother's room, I see that he has woken up a fly. So I eat him.

Emily Lewis, mentor

I wrote this piece while working with my mentee during a weekly mentoring session. We were writing about GREEN.

A Single Blade

A single blade of grass brings him to attention, whispering her call to come. He cocks his head and listens for the sharp whistle. He's aware of the physics behind the sound, of course – hot air forced past a long, tender shoot pressed between two delicate fingers and resting against the softest lips he has ever kissed. What he can't figure out is how only she can make nature sing in such a way that it pierces his heart and makes him know, without question, exactly where he belongs.

He smiles as he hears the call echo through the valley again, more shrill this time, vibrating the air with her insistent plea. He climbs up from his aching knees, brushing the day's grime from the crevices and wrinkles in which it has collected, and heads across the green pasture, toward the sound, toward home.

When I was younger, I was in awe of The Blue Man Group banners that were hung in the hotel lobbies of Las Vegas.

All Things Blue

You may call me by my first name, first name only. The name is Clarence.

I have a little fetish for all things blue. I have a particular shade of robin's-egg blue shirt for each day of the week. My dress pants must be pressed and ironed. My pots and pans must be neatly hung in my kitchen in order of size, above the sink. My cereal must only be the blue-boxed organic corn flakes, and my milk blue-jugged, whole. I am a self-confessed perfectionist to the extreme. My nails must be cut every Tuesday night. I eat my meals at precisely the same time every day. My penmanship is precise, and I write in baby blue ink.

The Blue Man Group in Las Vegas makes my blue blood bounce. Even the ring I gave my fiancé was a sapphire with opals. I live near the ocean, so my outdoor view is blue. My minivan is navy blue and so is my hair. If I could dye my skin like those people in *Avatar*, I would.

And let me tell you, I vow to never go to jail, because I don't ever want to wear those hideous neon orange jumpsuits, ever.

Alejandra Castillo, age 18

During a session with my mentor at a local park, she asked me to take off my shoes and walk barefoot on the grass. Who said writing can't be fun?

Rebel

Don't encourage me
To take off my shoes
And run like a wild beast
Across fields of Irish green
No, don't dare me

I'm already running
Towards the field
And if I move fast enough
The grass tickles
My pale foot playfully

If I suddenly slow down
I sense a mystery
Under the ground my toes embrace
Somewhere, real low
An anonymous creature crawls

It gives me nightmares
But soon
The cold northern wind
Washes away my fear
And I dance

These leafy spikes transform
Into rivers of cool, dark water
Mud, intrusive between my toes
Does not bother me
You do not bother me

Now you'll forever wonder what it's like
To run barefoot on sheets of Irish grass

~~#~~Write yourself out of your comfort zone; write in an unfamiliar genre.

Kim Genkinger, mentor

When I was working with my mentee, we talked about color showing up in unexpected places. As we were writing, I was looking out over concrete-covered Los Angeles — so beige. It made me mourn for living things, like grass.

Still Standing

Still standing, a lone soldier
bravely at attention
amid the concrete ruins that stretch
beyond the horizon at eye level.

His green, exposed body
vulnerable
to the sun's life-sucking rays.

He cannot move, roots anchoring him
into the packed earth, aching
to be quenched by something more nourishing
than the destruction of progress.

Nichelle Downs, age 15

Thinking of life and the beautiful colors of the sky and the earth inspired this piece.

Blue

I say hello to the blue sky
You live in a little town
Where all you see is frowns

These skies
They live sadly
A blue life

They are filled with clouds
These feelings
Bring forth a melody

Sometimes it feels wrong
When I sing a sad song
But you brighten the day

When I sing a fast song
These clouds
Make me feel okay

Gisel Julia Saumat, mentor

*I remember a shirt my ex-boyfriend used to wear and how
it reflected his personality and what transpired between us.*

Plaid Green Shirt

He wore it almost every day
The same old plaid green shirt

He's wearing it in pictures
With his other love before me
He's wearing it in pictures
Of us together, when we were in love

That horrible night
One I wish I could forget
He was wearing that plaid green shirt
Now I imagine it torn into pieces

Once we got back together
We were going to make it work
I bought him a new version
Of that plaid green shirt

It couldn't change the direction
Our love would go
He would never change
Who he was for me

Maybe one day
He will look at his plaid green shirt
And think of
What we should have been

Blue

I was feeling down
I wanted to be still
Not make a sound
Feeling down

I wanted my eyes shut
I wanted to be lost
To be cold
Without him there

At the place
I called home
I had no hope
If I went back there

Instead I cope
With the disappearance
Of my heart
I was feeling down

Blue

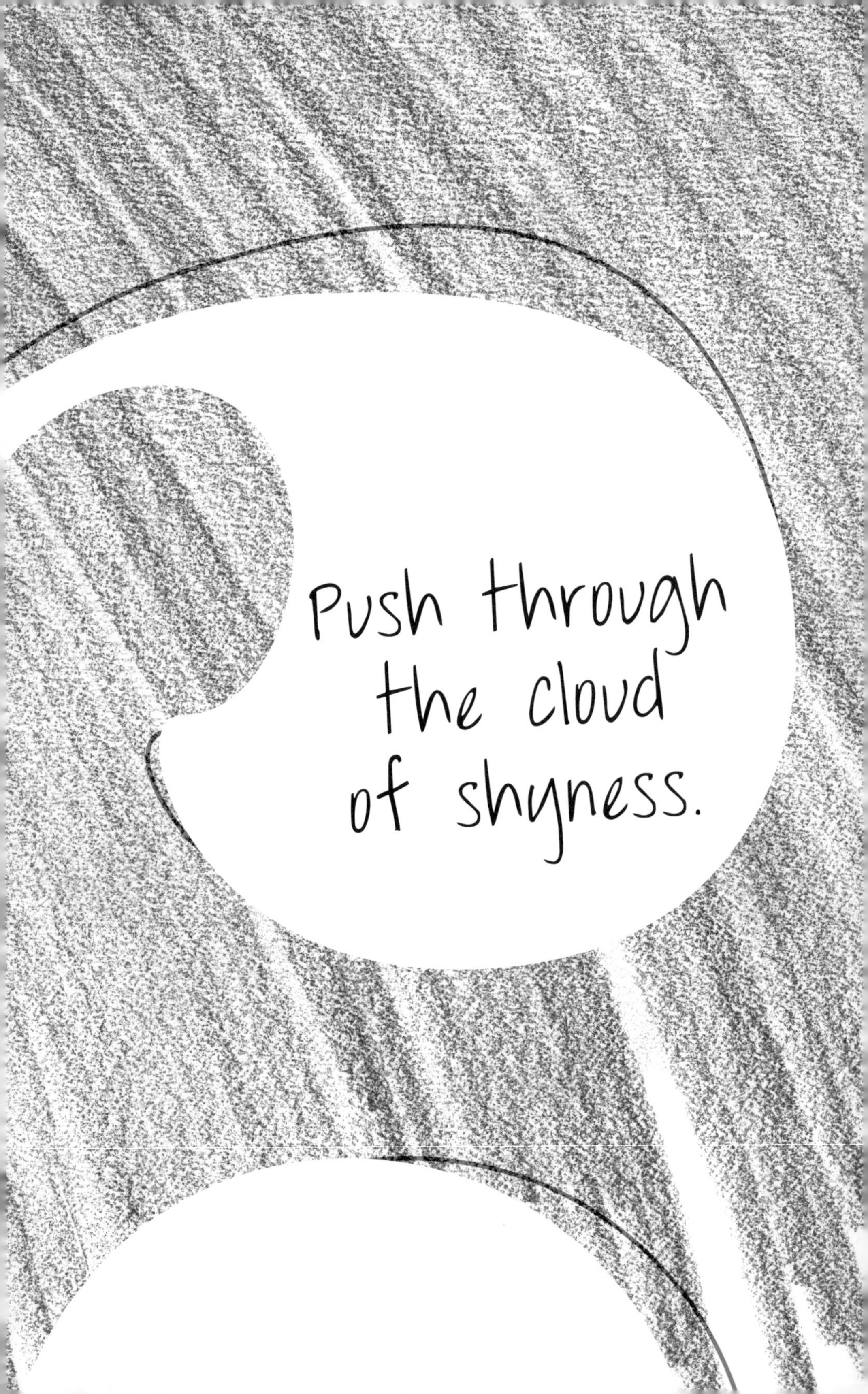
Push through the cloud of shyness.

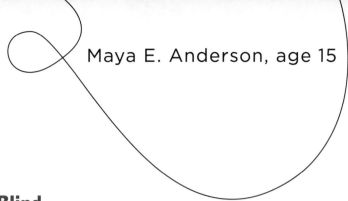

Maya E. Anderson, age 15

Love Is Blind

Is it possible
the first time you saw me
you thought
I looked beautiful?

Be honest.
I remember that disgusting emerald green shirt,
holey blue jeans and brown flip-flops,
and let's not mention my hair!

Whenever I ask you,
"When did you know I was the one?"
You say, "I knew the first time
I laid eyes on you."

Well – I'm breaking up with you,
because as sweet and romantic
as that sounds,
I'm just not convinced!

(Mystery)

Behind the
Glass

Jump into the scene of the crime — start a story from the middle and don't leave out any details.

Ariana Rodriguez, age 17

*I felt compelled to write a story
with an unreliable narrator.*

Sound of Silence

"My typewriter came to life!" I exclaimed ecstatically.

"Well, don't worry," my mother sighed. "You'll be committed soon. I'll send you the paperwork."

There was a click and I hung up the phone in utter frustration. I turned to look at my new personified friend. I had been preoccupied by my pointless phone call and hadn't noticed that it had left the room. Though I assumed it was impossible for it to have traveled up the stairs, I found its trail of cobwebs telling me otherwise.

I ran up the two wooden flights of stairs and entered the library. It was nowhere in sight. I walked into another room and had a strange sensation that I should return to the library. There it was in the center of the room, waiting for me. A sheet of paper was rolled inside with one typed word in the center: "Paperwork?"

Completely puzzled, I did not know whether to laugh or shriek in horror. I placed my trembling fingers on the keys, but they wouldn't budge and became rigid and hard. Thinking the keys were just jammed, I tried again. This time, I felt an impenetrable shield that would not let me break through. When I lifted my fingers, the keys clicked and clacked like a round of gunfire, until "Do not touch!!!" was typed on the page. Infuriated, I pressed the keys down so roughly, I almost snapped my fingers off.

My eyes narrowed and my jaw clenched. I sat on the floor, staring directly at the typewriter, prohibiting myself from blinking, the tension building and my pulse racing. Without any acute mental awareness, I rose, walked outside, and returned with an ax — but the hunk of metal that was supposed to be waiting for me was gone.

Ashlee Polarek, age 17

It was raining and, in my imagination, I saw a girl running. I had to find out where she was going.

Anywhere

She clutches the sopping wet hoodie to her chest and races down the dimly lit street. Murky puddles soak her black Vans and raindrops blur her vision. She stops to check the time and fix the messenger bag slipping off her shoulder. Goosebumps cover her exposed wrist. She moves her plastered blond hair out of her eyes and takes off again.

Her heavy breathing and footsteps pierce the deafening silence. The train is leaving soon. She can't miss it.

She stumbles into the train station and pulls fifteen limp dollars out of her pocket. She slides them under the ticket window.

"Where to, sweetie?" asks the elderly woman from behind the glass.

She glances nervously over her shoulder, relieved no one has followed. She slowly lowers her hood.

"Anywhere," she replies.

Yvonne Ha, age 18

Serendipity

The wind whipped violently around me, lashing my hair against my face. In the bright sunlight, I had to squint, even with my goggles on. The straps dug into the back of my head, but I didn't bother fixing them. At such a high altitude, the gusts felt cold against my arms; colder than the metal bar I was resting on.

I stared out at the distance, watching as the landscape below passed by. I didn't feel like looking back to Sanburydow.

"Don't look so distressed, Jeremy. I'm positive that one day, the four of us will meet again."

Josephine's words filtered through my mind, making the void in me even bigger. I took in a lungful of cold air and let it burn my throat.

The metal door on the side of the airship opened and shut. I turned to look at Lewis approaching. His lips were set in a grim line, the same as mine. He stepped by me and mirrored my stance. We watched each other without attempting to talk. Speaking was difficult due to the fast winds.

After a while, he turned to me and mouthed, "We finally made it." I nodded, a sour victory welling in my chest. I closed my eyes.

The winds continued howling around us.

Shazé Williams, age 16

*Riding the bus from school in the evenings
inspired me to start this piece.*

On Crenshaw

She left the baby behind
Her amnesiac mind
Damned with guilt
When she told the bus driver to stop

Each time she yelled
There was no response
Suddenly the bus
Came to an immediate stop

She fell down
But got back up
And ran out the door
Into oncoming traffic

The baby sat there
Eyeing the passengers
He was a smart, gentle baby
He had learned one thing

"Stay where you are
And do not move"
Mom came running back
She hadn't gone far

That was the day
She became so attached
To her baby son
She could not let him go

Rosa Palermo, age 17

In this excerpt, the two main characters have just crossed a bridge to the other side of Elodea and are looking for a bag of gems, the currency in this fantastical land.

The Green Gems (an excerpt)

Zarya and Aric walked across the bridge, arriving in the jungle. It was dark, humid and crowded with vines and thick trees. The morning also brought a fog seeping in through the trees. They walked to a hill that dropped steeply into fallen trees. It was a place most would usually avoid, but seemed to be a perfect hiding place for the gems. Aric climbed downhill and looked under the fallen trees.

"Are you sure it's here?" he called, after checking under the third fallen tree.

"That's what the map says. It's in a gray woven bag," answered Zarya.

Aric continued to look, without luck. The spirits were smart and wouldn't leave it on the ground where any animal could find it.

"Wouldn't they hide it up in the trees?" he asked.

Aric knew that he would hide the bag there if he were given the task. Hugging and squirming up a tree, he got to a branch with a nest at the end. The thick branch quickly thinned as it got further away from the trunk. Aric thought if he moved quickly, he could run back in time before the branch cracked.

He ran, and sure enough, the green gems were there. Grabbing them, he started to head back, but he wasn't fast enough. He fell, along with the branch, to the forest floor, causing the dead leaves to fly up in the air, making his descent look like a grand finale stunt. Zarya laughed at Aric's "performance."

Once the leaves had cleared, Aric grumbled, "You could have gotten it a lot easier, couldn't you?"

"Yep," Zarya smirked, "but you didn't ask."

Rachel Fain, mentor

*My mentee Cassie and I each used the rare book stacks
at the Huntington Library as the setting for a scene.*

Those Meddling Kids,
with Apologies to Scooby Doo

"Did you hear that?"

"No."

"What?"

"Shh! I'm listening!" Claudia hissed.

They all froze. The air conditioning hummed. There was a faint buzz from the overhead lighting.

Adam shrugged. "Nope. I must have imagined it."

Claudia glared at him. Jane looked thoughtful. "What did it sound like?"

"I don't know…maybe like a scrapey-thud. Or a jingle-smack. Or maybe a whiffle-whump?"

"Dude," said Mitchell. "I hear that all the time."

The others turned to Mitchell, expectant. He smiled and blinked at them blankly. Jane prompted, "And…"

"Huh? Oh! It's the sound my bike makes whenever I take a spill on the boardwalk."

"Did you fall off your bike a few minutes ago?" asked Claudia.

"Uh, no. I don't have—"

"And do you think someone else might —"

Adam cut in. "Claud, leave him alone."

"What? I'm just trying to establish —"

"It's okay, man. She's right. If there is someone riding a bike in here, they're in loads more trouble than we are."

"That's not what I —"

"Shh! I heard it – the whiffle-whump." Jane's voice was a barely audible squeak. "Sounds like Marley's Ghost is walking around wrapped in chains, only…if Marley were made of books."

"Yes! That's it exactly!" said Adam.

Whiffle-whump. The sound caught Claudia mid-eye-roll. "No way…"

"Way."

"Um, dudes? You know that mummy's curse thing? The one I told you about? The one you all laughed at?"

"Mitchell, you saw that in a cartoon! And that library was in Alexandria – in Egypt!"

"Yeah, but you said the Alexandria library was destroyed a while ago, and that sign back there said this one has lots of scrolls and stuff, just like the cartoon."

Whiffle-whump! It was getting closer. Wide-eyed, they looked at each other, before screaming and scrambling for the nearest exit, each in a different direction.

Jane Gov, mentor

This is a scene from a novel I am working on.

The Chase (an excerpt)

Ainslie lost track of how long she had been running. Her legs ached and she was breathing hard. Her wood-brown hair was drenched, tangled, and whipped around her neck. She winced as she forced her legs further, shoes squishing into mud puddles, branches slapping her frozen face. She was just starting to wonder if she was going the wrong way when she saw the glow from the lamppost. She breathed a sigh of relief. Home.

She burst through the front door and locked it. She held her breath. A flicker of outside light told her something or someone had swept past. Two shadows reflected against one of the windows. "No," she breathed.

Slowly, she tried to edge away from the front door but slipped, lurching forward. She grabbed a nearby table to steady herself, cursing her clumsiness. They had heard her.

"Ainslie?" Clare's voice called from behind the door. "Ainslie, we can explain." Clare's voice was growing frantic. "Please, please open the door."

Ainslie hesitated. Her grandfather's words echoed in her memory: "They'll think you belong to them." But what did he say after that?

"Ainslie!" This time it was a male's voice. Gilan. His voice was forceful. "Open this door!"

Crrrrack!

A tree had fallen, or it may have been the howl of the wind. Ainslie couldn't tell. She backed further away from the door. At the foot of the stairs, she glanced up. The polished banister gleamed at her in the half-light. But there was something else. Large, wet footsteps were imprinted on the wooden stairs. A chill ran up Ainslie's spine.

Someone was inside.

Natasha Billawala, mentor

*I have always had a fear of being chased and
this was my attempt to express that horror.*

Chased

My heart pounds and sinks
A bitter taste consumes me
I run to safety, but it eludes

Someone, something
Crazy-sick, pursues
With one intent, to hurt me

A door ahead is hope
If I can make it inside, inside, inside
Almost there

A rush of anxiety
My skin prickles and itches
I slam the door

But that someone
Something
Pushes back

A tug of war but finally I win
The deadbolt secure
I breathe again

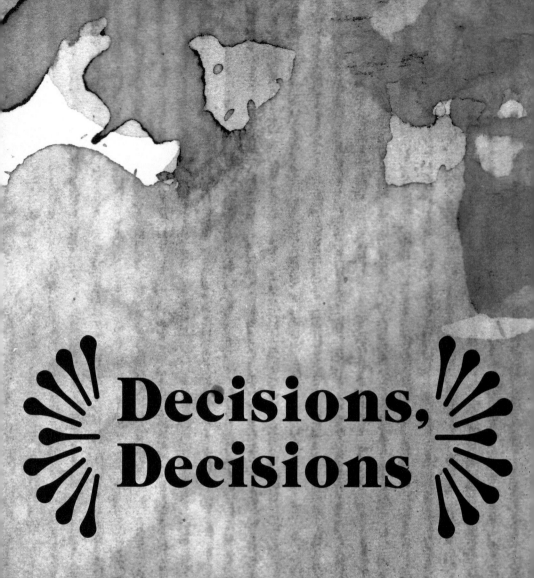

Decisions, Decisions

(Teen Life/ Growing Up)

Revise, revise, revise.

This piece was inspired by drama and how I try to deal with it — by meditating and sleeping.

Decisions, Decisions

Midnight phone conversation with the voicemail.

"*Beep*…I'm sorry, I never meant for this to happen."

The room is cold and quiet. Wind whistling. Salty tears disappear on my satin pillow as I gaze up at the ceiling. I find myself thinking about the good times. Those days were much better. I whisper to myself, "It's going to be okay."

My fingers trace hearts on the foggy window over and over. My head is pounding. If only I could escape this drama. My fairytale dreams would become reality.

Eyes closed, I wish away all the negativity and drift into a place where it's only me and serenity.

Yamuna Haroutunian, age 18

*When my mentor and I meet, we use the first few
minutes to freewrite. This emerged from one of those sessions.*

Glazed and Glorious

We are skinny teenagers with bad, foofy hair, sitting at the kitchen table
around a box of Krispy Kremes. It's that kind of morning when the sun is like
butter and it's just cool enough for pajama pants and just warm enough for
a tank top. The TV in the background babbles about scandals and oddities
that happened thousands of miles away, but no one moves to turn it off. The
useless noise in the background only amplifies the conversation that happens
here, the one that matters, like a harmony of cacophony, in the key of glazed
and glorious.

When we remember these days, we will remember the strange but perfect
details – the headline "Arcadia Girl Continues to Impress," and the photo
underneath of a crazy-haired girl with a warm, toothy grin, the suddenly
beautiful taste of orange juice, the fact that it is a Monday and the rest of the
week seems to stretch into the future, like a pleasant summer month.

Ashley Soltero, age 14

The Journey Begins

Forced to put up a front,
to act like someone I wasn't
when wrong always seemed right
and it was easier to do the irrational,
my adrenaline would speed up,
intense.

Might as well get used to this lifestyle
and my so-called friends.

Write because
you have a real
passion for it and
because you can.

Cindy Collins, mentor

This is an excerpt from a novel I'm writing.

The Ride (an excerpt)

Melba sat on a scratchy chair in the fluorescent glare of the camp nurse's office and picked at the fresh bandage on her knee. The nurse had cleaned the wound with rubbing alcohol and a few pale streaks ran down to her ankle. At one point, two of the streaks crossed, forming a misshapen "X" along her dusty calf.

Melba stared at her leg and contemplated all of the "X" words she knew. Xanthe, X-ray, xerif, also spelled shereef, not to be confused with the English word "sheriff." The icy feeling in the pit of her stomach began to grow. She wondered how much trouble she was actually in, even though she'd really only borrowed the horse. And not even.

Technically, she'd really only sat on him. Maybe she'd whispered "let's go" in his ear, but had that really worked? Had she made the horse gallop across the crowded volleyball court, or had he done it on his own? Had she made him jump the fence at the parking lot or was she just along for the ride? Before she knew it, they were rounding the bend that led to the beach trail along the cliff. She imagined skimming the white caps all the way to the horizon.

A crashing wave boomed below. She looked down and saw the horse's hooves pounding the dirt trail, her hands clutching the reins, the large shadow of the horse with her small one perched on top, bouncing along on the ground beside them. And that's when it hit her: "I don't know how to ride a horse," she thought. And that's when she fell.

"Melba, are you listening to me?" the nurse asked. She was a hundred years old or so, with a soft, fuzzy face that crinkled whether she smiled or frowned. Mostly, Melba had seen her frown. "You're lucky you weren't killed out there today. What happened?"

Melba wiped the "X" off her calf. "I looked down."

Reconfigured

Adolescence, my rebirth,
the carefree child knows who they are,
the teenager is an enigma of self.
You turn the hourglass on its head,
and watch as the grains rearrange.
You will never be the same.

Adolescence, my purgatory,
anxiety in piles of strife and worry.
The teenager endures this cruel initiation,
for the benefit of their soul's recreation.
Leave it all behind, mountains of dirt.
You'll never be the same.
We will never be the same.

Adolescence, my journey to acceptance.
I am the teenager, reconfigured into the person I will forever be.
A powerful force, the reflection of my hopes and dreams.
Forget what I've been told, wanderlust is not aimlessness.
I will never be the same.
I'll be better.

Rachel Torres, mentor

Talking to the brilliant (and young!) teens of WriteGirl helps me remember when I was a very intense teenager, and everything had a desperate, cosmic tinge.

Keys, Dangling

"Maybe," she sighs.

Yes! That's me! Already in the car, rolling down the squeaky windows and turning up the music, fresh wind and hot setting sun on my cheeks.

"Well…" she says.

Oh, no. No. This is me – trapped at home, not allowed to take the car out, rummaging for food in the pantry, thumbing the never-ending scroll of status updates. Greasy, hot cheese on a microwaved pizza bagel – this will be my evening.

"Did you finish your homework?"

(It's just Saturday, but she won't care.)

"I've done at least half," I say. There's all day tomorrow to be old and indoors! I want to be out tonight, to be young.

"Where will you go?" she asks, and in this instant, my entire future diverges before me, split by a long, smooth seam, joined only at the beginning by the car keys dangling off the tip of my mom's index finger. The key fob has a tiny silver bell, and it tinkles, laughing at me. Either I'm going out because I get the car, and I pick up my very best friend and we eat burritos, and laugh, and drive by Adam's house, and be young and carefree forever, or I stay home on a Saturday night, no car, and have to do the other half of my homework while my mom goes out with her book club. I'll be old and tired and never learn to have any fun, or drive aimlessly down suburban streets at night, with the soft hush of leafy trees and winking stars witnessing me in my youth.

"Well," she sighs…

Elda Pineda, mentor

The Pegasus

Susie and her mother had a terrible row the week before her birthday. Mrs. Fluffenbottom had certain ideas about the way a young squirrel like Susie should behave. Susie wanted to spend her birthday at the playground, but her mother insisted on having a party at home, with a proper acorn cake and pink punch, consumed from the good china.

Susie would prefer to wear overalls, but her mother would rather she wear a starched pinafore and Mary Janes with knee socks. But these were everyday arguments heard around breakfast tables all over world. Today's extraordinary quarrel was about a birthday present. Susie Fluffenbottom wanted a bicycle.

Squirrels in Nicenberry did not own bicycles and they certainly did not have the one that Susie had her eye on. Named "The Pegasus," it was emerald green with a white leather seat, a rattan basket, a tinkle-y bell and glorious yellow and green streamers on the handlebars. She saw it in a shop window on Hennepin Avenue and was instantly enamored.

"The Pegasus" became the center of all her daydreams. Often, when she was supposed to be washing dishes or tidying her drey, she would imagine herself flying through the city streets atop her bicycle, fur smoothed back by the wind, the envy of Minneapolis.

Susie burst into tears and scampered off to cry alone on her bed when Mrs. Fluffenbottom told her it was unladylike for squirrels to ride bicycles. Wouldn't she enjoy a new dress instead, perhaps with a matching hat?

It would break her mother's heart to say that bicycles were only for humans. While a year older in one week, her daughter was not old enough for the knowledge that a squirrel will bear many disappointments throughout life. Bicycles were only the first.

Tiffany Tsou, age 14

I wrote this at the WriteGirl Fiction Workshop using the "Amazing Race" writing prompts, which asked us to write about a character who missed class.

Please Wake Up on Time

BEEP BEEP* BEEP*

"What's that noise?" I toss and turn in my bed, but the beeping does not cease.

"Oh no! It's 8:00! I'm going to be late!" I jump out of bed, wondering where my mother is. I scramble to brush my teeth and hair.

At the breakfast table, I see a note left behind: "Had to leave early. Take yourself to school." I look at the clock again: 8:37. I've already missed first period. Whatever. It's Friday anyway! Wait… What's the date?! It's the last day of finals week – I just missed half of my math final!

I hop into my car and drive to school, park horribly at the curb, and sprint into the building. I run to room A251, panting. I open the door, noticing that everyone in class continues to look down at their tests. Ms. Sharp gives me a stern look. "You're late."

I take my seat next to Daniel, the cutest guy in class. He looks at me and smiles while I try to hide my blushing cheeks. I reach to my side, trying to take off my backpack straps, but I can't seem to find them resting on my shoulders. Did I forget my backpack at home? I look around to see if anyone has noticed.

Everyone stops taking their finals and looks in my direction. I turn my attention to Daniel, who also stares at me. Is there something wrong? Daniel stands up and walks over to me, smiling. He leans into my face, but not for a kiss. Instead, he whispers in my ear, "Nice slippers."

I look down, mortified. I am still in my pajamas! And out of all of them, I chose the Hannah Montana set, with bunny slippers and green-toed socks to match.

Nancy Lara, age 15

I wrote this poem because I saw a woman who had the most beautiful hair in the world – I loved it so much I had to write about how it might feel to have it.

The Hair

Old rusty woman
Has something precious
I need and want

Her fancy smooth
Black hair
Glamorizes the room

The bottom is curly
The top is like an afro
But it doesn't reach for the sky

Its shape is like a cloud
On a woman who doesn't
Need it – it doesn't even go with her

How I want it
She must shave it off and give it to me
And I'll show it off to the world!

Then, I'll finally be happy

Melanie Ballesteros, age 15

In this piece, ants are the thoughts you don't want to think about that always seem to pop into your head at the wrong time. I've had trouble with these ants, but I know with God's help, I can defeat them.

The Insecticide for Ants

Thoughts are like friends
who influence me
in ways good and bad

They can help me
or be against me
or confuse my mind

They torture me
like bullies
but I'm protected

by the Spirit, the One
who gave me the power
to control my thoughts

Because of this
I sleep
falling into the couch

Kissing my nephew
Sweet and sticky cheeks
Oh my

Gabriella Evans, age 17

I wrote this poem after finishing a book I had been reading for a while.
There was no sequel to the book, so when it ended, the friendship the main
character and I had developed was over with the turn of a page.

Friends

I'm the girl
The world doesn't notice
The one you think has no friends

But I am not alone
My companions
Are always close

I keep them in my backpack
I keep them in my bedroom
They will never leave me

They whisper to me
"We will never hurt you"
"We will never betray you"

The pages crinkle
Paper absorbs
The sweat from my palms

Words smudge
The ink is permanent
It cannot be erased

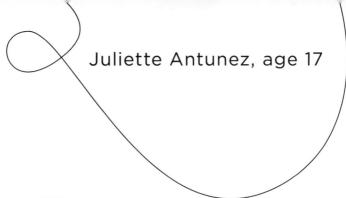

Juliette Antunez, age 17

Come A Long Way

My life began in the beautiful tropical country of Honduras. I remember the warm breeze and my grandma's soft, delicate hands caressing my face. I can still hear my aunts' and cousins' loud chuckles of laughter. My family taught me the values that have remained with me. They are the standing army that won't let me fall.

When I was seven, my mom and I came to Los Angeles to reunite with my dad. Knowing I had to leave the people I loved completely tore me apart, but part of me was joyous to know I would be with my dad again.

My first day of elementary school in Los Angeles was unforgettable. I was a terrified, lonely girl on the gigantic, yellow bus full of strangers. I cried my eyes out, clearing my tears away with my dark brown sleeve. I received extra help so I could learn English, and that's when my passion for writing began.

In third grade I had an opportunity to read one of my poems at UCLA. As I began reading my poem, I realized I had come a long way from the petrified little girl I used to be.

I have a vision of myself as an international journalist. I want to see the world from different perspectives while learning about myself. I want to see everything life has to offer.

(family)

I BORROW ALL YOUR CLOTHES

Write when you're
inspired by others.
Write to _inspire_ others.

This piece was written during the WriteGirl Poetry Workshop.
I was thinking of my little sister.

Lion Heart

My little sister,
like a lion with her golden hair.
She wakes up grumpy,
roaring for food.

Her little head
heavy
with numbers
and words.

She is
a little piece
of my heart,
but wants the lion's share.

Nobody can say no to her jade green eyes.

Ciara Blackwell, age 16

When my aunt passed away, I thought about what she was like and the positive energy she brought into my life.

Free Spirit

You are free!
Free from all inhibitions
Free from your troubles
Spread your wings and fly
Fly to the top of the heavens
Fly with our ancestors
While they tell old African stories
Let your hair loose and shout to the world
Shout to this planet we call Earth
Where the sun shines
Stretch your love
Stretch out to me
You are free
Spirited Woman

I wrote this piece to express the love and admiration I have for my mother.
I don't show it as much as I should.

An Unshakeable Love

I'm not always nice
I fuss and shout
Say things
I don't mean

I tell you
To leave my room
But deep down inside
I want you to stay

I get on your nerves
Make you mad
And through all that
Your love is strong

I borrow all your clothes
And your shoes
Please don't get me started
On your food

Through all
The high school drama
Arguments I don't even remember
You're my mom; I'm your daughter

Sometimes I'm lazy
Sometimes I'm slow
But when I feel like giving up
You remind me of God's plan

At times I think to myself
I am really blessed
At times like this
I know your love is strong

Jenny Sheng, age 17

My sister's name is Joy, and she truly lives up to her name.
She's seven years older than I and left for college when I was in the
sixth grade. Whenever Joy comes home, I feel like I've been reborn.

Your Sunshine

The night is damp, cold
And your light is not upon me
How do I continue
With such little warmth inside
Without you
I'm surrounded by darkness

Even though
You are so far away
And out of reach
Just seeing you for a moment
Would lift my spirits
This moon without its sun

But I'll keep moving on
Circling round and round
Blinded
Hoping one day
Your light
Will dawn upon me

Danielle Nicole Knox, age 15

I was thinking about how words can express deep feelings or funny, silly things. This piece was written for my mom.

Wishes

If I could make
A wish for you
All of your days
Would be shining bright

All of your money
Would grow on trees

All of your time
Would never be late

If I could make
A wish for you
All of your mistakes
Would be lessons learned

All of your happiness
Would never fade

If I could make
A wish for you
There are so many
Things I'd do

Rachel Hogue, mentor

This piece was inspired by a poem in Rita Dove's poetry collection
Thomas and Beulah. *I wrote it in honor of my grandmother.*

She Is Dreaming

She is dreaming:
  of trains again
  of motor car malfunctions
  of faulty brakes
  of collision crashes
She is remembering:
  the trip out west
  the millionth cooked meal
  the sunday sermons
  the school day subjects
She is talking about:
  children's homes
  flirtatious french pen pals
  great depressions & world wars
  factories
  grandpa
  jesus
She was:
  here
now
  gone

I wrote this at the WriteGirl Poetry Workshop. I based it on a picture of a man standing with a ridiculous amount of balloons in his hand in the middle of a busy street. Everyone was looking his way.

Balloon Circus

People will take notice of this floating circus.
"John," they'll say, "What is all this?"
"They're for her. One for everything about her."

I like the zebra-striped one the best.
It tickles my shoulder
As it bounces against the others.

So many colors, like a light show above my head.

I'm sure she'll like the fish.
Decorated with blue and green scales.
Or maybe she'll favor the bunny, ears at the top.

The bouquet sparkling like snow on a mountain.

"I would have bought more, but I ran out of money."
They'll laugh, and I'll smile
feeling like the best father in the world.

Kezia Obasi, age 14

My creative juices were flowing and I was inspired to write about two guy cousins who are really close, yet so different!

My Cousin Chris

It's rare that my cousin Chris is allowed to come over to my house, but when he does, it's nonstop entertainment. Chris and I are like best friends, so I guess that makes us…"frelatives."

Chris is good-looking and the star of the basketball team. He's the most aggressive player on the court and the smoothest off. We're both sixteen, but he's a month older and never lets me forget it.

He says I talk too fast; I think he listens too slowly. I'm the kind of guy who can't stand even a drop of mud on my new kicks. Chris would live in the dirt if he could.

We compete at everything from who can shoot snot out the farthest to who can get the most digits at the mall. Chris and I have been going at it since we were little, and nothing I do changes the fact that he always comes out on top – but today is going to be different.

Today is the *Obstacle Course 2011*, the granddaddy of all obstacle courses. We start with our bikes at the mailbox, then we see who can do the longest wheelie down the block. The winner is the one who touches Ms. Brown's dog, Spike, first. He's a hideous, gray pit bull with beady eyes who won't hesitate to rip a kid's arm off.

If I win, I get Chris's precious basketball cards. Honestly, I couldn't care less about them. I just know it would kill him. If he wins, he gets my Xbox; he's been eyeing it since Christmas.

I might have lost a bet to Chris once or twice. Okay, I lose most of our bets, but today's different because I found my lucky green socks. Shhh…

Sara Kimura, age 16

*I wrote this at the WriteGirl Fiction Workshop.
It is part of a story about a girl named Alexandria.*

A Clean Slate

I got up out of bed and stumbled to the kitchen. It was the first place I went every morning – the first place I saw when I woke up. I sat down at the table and put my head down – the table was as cool and smooth as it could only be this early in the morning when nobody else was up yet.

Throughout the day, all sorts of crumbs, drinks, sauces, and art supplies decorated the table. But each night, just before bed, the table was cleared off and wiped down with the yellow/green sponge. The only things that wouldn't budge were the scuffs and scrapes that come with a household of five. They give the table character, like the scrapes on the surface of my heart.

(Food)

Odd
Concoction

Samantha Nagle, age 15

*At the very first workshop, we each selected two Post-It Notes
with secret words on them. My two said "disappointed" and
"during dinner." This instantly reminded me of the times when
I had to submit to eating leftovers.*

Disappointed During Dinner

The single question that gives us hope
of herb-roasted lamb and juicy steaks:
"What's for dinner?"

After my labor, the fruit
at the day's sweet end
makes my afternoon's hunger worthwhile.

The ends that justify the means,
the sustenance that we receive
to replenish and renew.

The answer makes us spiral down
to the reality of soggy pizza and chewy chicken:
"Leftovers."

And so disappointment is my dinner.

Christina Gabrielle Anderson, age 18

*I wrote this during the WriteGirl
Season Kickoff event at the poetry table.*

Fortune Cookie

What's inside
Could tell my future
Or may tell me a lie

Will I have the love
I always wanted
Or is love not worth the try

"You will walk on the soil
Of many countries"
Is what it said inside

It's not what I believe
But time will allow me to understand
And tell me what I want to hear

Zzzahkia Burnley, age 14

Intrigued with a Spoon

A spoon can scoop up
all the joy and happiness
there is in life.

A spoon is a gift of life.
A spoon scoops up joy
as well as happiness.

Joy and happiness
are the keys to life
and life is the key
to eternal happiness.

Kathleen DiPerna, mentor

I wrote this piece during my weekly meeting with my mentee, Danielle. We both wrote about the theme of Green and Blue. She wrote about beautiful leaves and water and snow and I wrote about asparagus. Oddly enough, both of our pieces were about our love of family.

Asparagus Through Rose-Colored Eyes

"Asparagus Patties" might be the most unappealing name given to a treasured family dish. For most, the term doesn't inspire visions of festive plates being passed around a holiday table, with yummy moans of hunger or enthusiastic pleas for more. Hardly. Pair the word asparagus with the word patty and you'll likely hear, "Yuck, that sounds gross."

On its own, asparagus already struggles a bit with mass appeal. It's a bright green vegetable in the shape of stalky, aggressive-looking spears. Sure, it can be sautéed or grilled to fancy it up, but at the end of the day, it's a vegetable that is somewhat famously known for its ability to change the scent of one's urine. Not the most elegant correlation. Add the word "patty" to the end of it and sneering ensues.

Canned, wet asparagus spears mashed into messy little blobs with other special secret ingredients (including egg, breadcrumbs and freshly-grated Romano cheese), fried up in a pan of olive oil into thin, silver dollar-sized patties – for me, this odd concoction is a dish of heaven, worthy of awe and celebration, a dish crafted with great love and perfection by my beloved grandmother, Rose.

As a little girl I was called "Rosie" because I shared my grandmother's blonde hair and blue-green eyes. In our exclusively brown-eyed, brown-haired Italian family, this was quite a thrill. Her eyes. Her delicate hands. For some reason, food never tasted as good as when she prepared it. Her Sunday gravy and meatballs still go unmatched. A holiday without her asparagus patties would feel like just another day. All the magic and color would be lost. I could never let that happen. Now, it's my hands that keep those greenly magical spirited patties alive at our table. Sneers or not, there are never any leftovers.

(Places)

The

Plan

Was

Perfect

Write to free people from limited perceptions. Show them how strange the world is.

Jackelyne Cuellar, age 16

*I went to San Francisco and missed Los Angeles
a lot more than I thought I would.*

I'm Far and Away

I stare out the window, hoping to see your sunny skies,
your skyscrapers tall as dinosaurs and your long, dark streets.
All I see ahead are road and hills —
I'm on the road to San Francisco, every second farther away from you.
I want to go home, I want to scream,
but no one will hear me on this deserted highway.

I miss the smell of different foods around every corner;
waiting for the Rapid in front of the Macy's Plaza,
trying to get home to Huntington Park;
screaming and roaring at the Lakers;
staring at Disney Concert Hall, trying to figure out its shape;
seeing the colorful murals all over the City of Angels.

Superman would have loved to fly over your streets.
As I arrive and stand atop the Golden Gate Bridge,
I search for you.
I'm far and away
but I know you're there
awaiting my return.

Keren Taylor, mentor

Traveling always brings me back to myself,
despite the myriad of challenges.

Map of Manhattan

The bamboo leaf pattern of the hotel carpet is a mandala of repetition. The forest color fades, gently, as it nears the elevator doors – years of passage have worn it down. In the elevator, I struggle to remember how to interpret the subway map – it seems an oversize platter of red, yellow, orange, green and blue spaghetti.

At Port Authority, I am all turned around. I don't know north, south, Hudson from East River, but I keep walking and find a flea market in Hell's Kitchen. Silver spoons, mannequin heads, full-length mink coats and colored-glass ashtrays mix with geometric African clothing and brass Indian buddhas. At an antiques stall, I pick up a rusty compass that wobbles inside a battered wooden frame – the barrel-chested merchant booms "sixty-five" to me, and I set it down, carefully.

On 34th Street and 9th Avenue, the concrete is so compacted you can see the individual rock particles that make up the asphalt matrix. It forms a landscape, a dying coral reef, a thunderous landslide, before the crosstown M34 bus roars over top of it, startling me back from the curb.

The Macy's star, set against a two-story crimson wall, is a mashup of perestroika and capitalism. I feel the icy air conditioning blasting from each store along the long blocks to the Broadway station, but I am not lured. I ignore all the neon and back-lit signs, challenging myself not to read any of them.

Descending steep stairs to the token booth, I hang onto the railing, trying not to jam my aching toes into the front of my shoes. It's another two levels down to the downtown B and D trains. I angle away from shoppers, tourists and locals with bags, bikes and boxes, and a woman with two milk-chocolate poodles poking out of her Chanel shoulder bag.

The train arrives in a gust of hot subway air and we pack together, avoiding eye contact, staring at the ads that scream at us from every wall, gripping the stainless poles to not lose balance. At Lafayette, we spill out onto the platform and head to the stairs, again. My shoes crush my heels with each step.

I emerge onto Houston Street at a gas station and nearly step into a gummy-gray puddle of unknown liquids. I lurch sideways off the curb and a yellow cab swerves to miss me, honking fiercely. I am out of step with New York City.

Four rugged cobblestone blocks south, I see my salvation: "Spring Wellness Inc. 30-minute foot massage Chinese Qi Gong." The timing is perfect – it's 30 minutes until Happy Hour in Manhattan, and all I need is my feet back.

Melissa Wong, mentor

I moved to Los Angeles 11 years ago to pursue a career in TV.
I wrote this piece to commemorate the home I left behind.

Looking Homeward

Can you take me
To a quiet cul-de-sac that smells of freshly mowed grass
With warm breezes that drift between cookie-cutter homes
Carrying the twang of country music blaring out of open garages?

Is this the way
To a kitchen thick with the scent of fried lumpia rolls
With pots full of adobo pork and rice sticky with coconut milk
Filling large plates that clink and clatter from busy spoons?

There's no place
Like parks packed with family, grills smoking with skewers and corn
With nearby beaches awash with *coquina* and broken shells
Stretching for miles underneath the wingspan of cawing gulls

I belong
Among orange blossoms and manatees drifting along the bay shore
With flamenco dancers, wannabe singers and karaoke machines
Providing the sappy soundtrack to my long-overdue homecoming

The only magic
to writing is to
sit your butt down
and do it.

write your first draft
so quickly that your
censor can't keep up.

*I wrote this poem while living in New York, and it
has always been one of my favorites. It reminds me of
one of the most amazing chapters of my life.*

Being 25 in New York

standing taller while walking down 125th street in harlem
where my grandfather grew up
and into the theresa hotel
where malcolm x, duke ellington, and fidel castro have all stayed
leaping and twirling, ballerina style, through the white boxes of chelsea
working long days and knowing what self-sufficiency feels like;
standing on a rooftop and wishing on the one new york star
bird-watching in central park with my students
and seeing the world through their seven-year-old eyes,
praying in a pew at riverside
where martin luther king once stood delivering "beyond vietnam;"
primping for dates with guys from wall street,
but still focused on myself being stimulated in a wednesday night class surrounded
by other women who love teaching and writing,
seeing the same mother of three on the express train at 6:45 every morning
and wondering how she does it,
kissing on the steps of the met
jogging with the current of the hudson down the west side highway
dancing with friends and belting out the chorus when the dj plays "living on a prayer,"
feeling so right living my dream;

I'm like a child drinking a thick milkshake through a straw
with inverted cheeks, working muscles you didn't even know cheeks had,
lips red from being pursed together so tightly
savoring, absorbing, remembering...
sucking these moments in with all my might so that they do not slip past me
unnoticed, and end in oblivion.

Jillian Davis, age 17

I was inspired to write this since I am going to be traveling a lot this summer. I thought it would be an interesting twist to have a character find the one thing she was looking for by doing (and not enjoying) something new.

Great Expectations

The Girl decided to try traveling. Her friends had done it, her parents had done it, and just about everyone in the movies had done it, so why not her? Surely it *must* be fun.

Tickets were purchased and time from work taken off. The Girl was ready to spend two weeks in New York City. She'd been saving a year for this trip and no expense was going to be spared: staying at the Plaza, seeing a Broadway show, and finding her Cary Grant at the top of the Empire State Building.

The plan was perfect. The arrival, on the other hand was poorly executed. The Girl had never been on a plane before and turned as green as the grass back home. She felt what she thought were sky earthquakes, but she learned it was called "turbulence." A kid kicked her seat the whole time.

Once she checked into her hotel, she finally received the treatment she thought she deserved. The food was rich, the staff welcoming, and the view beat anything else in the world.

But a week passed and still she had not met the man of her dreams. She sulked and frowned, and even shed a tear, taking the horrid plane home five days early.

The Girl slumped in the airport, waiting to retrieve her luggage, only to discover it was lost. She dragged herself to the lost luggage counter, where an attractive young man listened to her story and grinned. He handed over her suitcase and said, "Lucky, I've never been."

The Girl smiled just then, for she had traveled, hated it, and found love.

Allison Deegan, mentor

*This is a memory of arriving in China as an exchange student in 1984.
I was reminded of this day after seeing a photo of the new,
modern terminal at the Beijing Airport.*

China, Day One

The day we arrived there were soldiers all over the airport, machine guns draped across their backs like seasoned travelers with carry-on bags. As we emerged from the plane, they stopped only to eyeball our ragtag group of eight jet-lagged Westerners. Several of us were a little tipsy from drinking on the plane from Tokyo, for a variety of reasons including a little bit of terror of the unknown. As they often do, the machine guns hastened our sobriety.

We were the only people in what looked like a new facility. It was 1984 and the reality of entering a Communist country, an entirely different world, engulfed us. With all of its anticipated Orwellian associations and drabness, China was much more chilling than anything I could have imagined. It felt like there wasn't enough oxygen in the air.

Even for favored, invited guests like us, the zeal with which the soldiers tore apart my luggage turned out to be a harbinger of things to come. On our visas, they called us scholars, as if extending a hand in welcome, and then they confiscated my Polaroid camera and all the film I'd brought, along with one of two Sony Walkmans. I couldn't tell why they only took one, but it was the newer model. Only half of my cassette tapes made it back into my suitcase. Had they gone through them a little more carefully, my presumptive sedition would have been made clear – I had included a copy of Brian Eno's album, *Taking Tiger Mountain (By Strategy)*, his response to one of the "model" Chinese operas allowed to be performed during the Cultural Revolution. At the time, it seemed more prank than political statement, but I began to rethink that decision the minute I saw the soldiers.

With some of our possessions and all of our clothes intact, the warning of confiscated Levi's being thankfully unfounded, we huddled from the customs area to locate a driver who was supposed to be waiting for us. He was the only one there, holding a handwritten sign that read "Americans." Yes, we were the Americans, as would be pointed out (literally, with pointed fingers) on nearly a daily basis.

(Nature)

Deep Roots

Danielle E. Flores, age 14

I wrote this piece with my mentor at one of our meetings.
To me, it shows that no matter who you love or how your family is,
you're always going to have fall and winter surrounding you
until it's time for spring and summer to kick in.
Like all good things, though, it always has to end.

My Seasons

Down
Go the leaves.
Love drifts slowly to the ground.
Crunch. Under my feet.
Avoid the common path to you.
Fall surrounds me.

Drop
sinks the ice.
Memories trapped in the frozen lake.
Slip. Under my feet.
Lose my hope in everything.
Winter sets in.

Bloom
Sprout the flowers.
Longed-for dreams of family
Open up as a rose takes in the sun.
Slurp. It fills my heart.
Spring awakens me.

Splash
Come the waves
That carry me
To laughter in light blue water.
Swish. Everything is perfect.
Summer nourishes me.

Fall returns.
The cycle begins.
Again.

Come to your senses;
Use all five in
your writing. ~~[scribble]~~

Amy Epperhart, age 18

Ode to Constellations

Here I stand, watching wistfully
rooted to the earth below
wishing I could run away
and in the moonbeams stray
bringing to my blurry sight
a hero cloaked in velvet night
among the glittering stars.

From the east, Castor and Pollux rise
to strum upon lute and lyre
against the dusty, icy glow
and rusty gleam of Mars.

Just beyond those tragic brothers
a mother bear stalks her prey.
Close behind follows her little one –
a little midnight sun.
Sweet cub, playing on your midnight stage
so free without chains or cage.
Little bear, how lucky you are.

How great it seems
in a world so mystical
invincible, cold, immortal
to live among the stars.

Trina Gaynon, mentor

This came out of a mentoring session experiment based on Jane Kenyon's "Let Evening Come." Each of us described our favorite time of day in a specific location.

Under the Moon

Lean and mangy, teeth and tongue
showing, coyote ranges the high desert
alone – near noon, pacing the road
alongside a car, in search of scraps.

He wants to spend hot daylight hours
in the burrow he dug to provide shade.
He prefers moving through the dark,
his eyes sharper than his prey's.

With the sun gone, the world cools.
The sands pop with gophers and mice,
water ripples with deep-voiced frogs.
A vole skitters out of his reach.

The world cools and the scents
of sage and wild grasses cloak
his reek from the nervous cottontail
he waits, like a cat, to pounce on.

Write the story
that follows you,
the one that pops
into your head –
at the grocery,
while walking the dog,
or just before
you fall asleep.

Jalisa Francis, age 18

I was sitting beside a window in a quiet place. As I looked outside,
I saw various things that made my senses tingle with inspiration.

Outside My Window

As I look outside my window
I think about my sense of smell
Flowers in my garden
Sweet and heavenly
The aroma grabs my taste

As I look outside my window
I feel the cool, salty ocean breeze
Blowing on my face
I imagine walking
On warm white sand

As I look outside my window
I see children running free
Their sweet outdoor haven
Not a care about life
When they get older

Looking outside my window
I think about my sense of touch
How life is viewed and lived
How it feels to look
through my window

Cassandra Shima, age 15

I wrote this when Rachel, my mentor, asked me to write down every word I could think of when I thought of water.

Water =

Babbling + bubbling + streaming +
        shower + rain +
    pure + hydrogen + oxygen + life +
reflect + release +
        Wild + wet +
    sodden + tears + sorrows +
        Roaring + crash + anger + ferocity + fear + anguish +
            Freedom + newness +
grime + trapped + sinking +
    bubble + breathe + nature +
        curiosity + terror +
        paint + art + creation +
Mirror + reflection +

    Drip

Mystic + sparkle + magic + rainbow +

    Drop.

Hunter Phillips, mentor

This is a truncated version of a longer poem about perspective: perspective on war, on the environment, on history, on where the human race is heading, on what all WriteGirls might face in the future.

Extinction Event

a warring, symphonic suite
of non-verbal tweets
quick, like birds
ramming each other with unhinged words
regurgitating wars already threaded
through scarves of lives completely unedited
so history becomes a disappointing fake
not rich tapestry like Marie Antoinette,
who never actually said "Let them eat cake!"

retreating, retracting, revising to be right
in the silence of a loud argument
that single word gotten in edgewise
can be so awfully unwise
wars, these stupid things, sighhhhhhh…take so much energy
and the census taker's heartbeats are a tilt-a-whirl out of whack,
he knows the balance of power is powering down
down the throat, down the hatch, down the tube
that new age, plastic-surgery-enhanced, HD, 3D, Blu-ray, sting ray, boob tube

so the earth shrugs Her shoulder irritably against the itch
of bickering, scolding, blaming…rolls Her arctic eyes and thinks,
"Whatever." Because really, an extinction event only means
She'll be fine.
She'll be totally fine.

Jenna Burns, age 14

I was thinking of raindrops as people. I remembered something I heard at a WriteGirl workshop: avoid clichés.

A Storm is Coming

I'm starting
to lose   everyone
one by one
  drop by drop
they fall from the clouds
     and hit the ground
too fast
     for me
          to catch them.

almost like a cloudy sky

lately
I have not been
in my mind
but in fact
I've been
     floating
through others'
  minds
and it
     tastes
     slightly
     lightly

blue.

Jody Rosen Knower, mentor

I wrote this piece at the WriteGirl Poetry Workshop, using the prompt
"She wants the Adaline ." It's been a harsh winter back home in New York,
with several significant blizzards, and I was missing the snow.

She Wants the Snow

She wants the snow.
She wants the air to chill
and the skies to darken.
She wants the mercury
to dive sharply
down the glass.
She wants the sounds
of the city
to still
and soften,
muffled
by the delicate deluge
of frozen
lace.

Rachel Wimberly, mentor

There were prompt cards taped under our seats at the WriteGirl Poetry Workshop, and mine asked "Where do you want to go?" I decided to write about the wind – because it's always roaming about.

The Wind Has No Home

I read somewhere once
the wind is the only element
in nature with no home
constantly roaming the earth
from tall mountains to green valleys
to the endless skies to deep seas
I've spent my life doing the same
I feel a kinship with the wind
we swirl around the world
blowing fiercely here and there
unable to grow deep roots
not willing to be in one place
the wind always is wandering
and I'm along for the ride

Vivian Tran, age 13

Tree Story

The tall tree of Bella Terra stands bold and strong
surrounded by bushes, weak and small.
The tree tough as stone, still as earth,
stares down at cars that blow its leaves down the earth.
At sunset, lights flash, doors shut,
people dash to their cars.

The tree waves its leaves at the people.

Write what you feel
and feel what
you write.

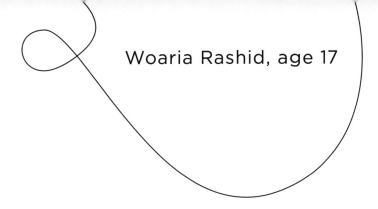

Woaria Rashid, age 17

Dazed

A pensive girl stood
Staring at an orchard tree
Spellbound as the sun hit her face
Dazed by the beauty of nature
That made her

Edna Cerritos, age 15

3-11-11

On March 11th, 2011, I am sitting in the kitchen doing my math homework with the biggest pain in my spine. I glance over to see the TV news.

A massive earthquake hits Japan. I'm scared. I don't know what to do. My heart breaks, and not even 20 minutes pass when a tsunami hits. I watch two people driving towards the water. They realize what it is and they do an immediate U-turn. A lot of homes are destroyed – my heart breaks into even more pieces.

I feel like leaving L.A. and going to help in Japan, but what can a 15-year-old girl do? If I could, I would help people evacuate. I start praying for everything to be okay. I pray for survivors.

I continue to watch TV. The nuclear plant is having a meltdown. I don't really understand, and I fear there won't be any place for the Japanese people to live.

What will Mother Nature look like now?

Kathi Bolton-Ford, age 16

I wrote this during the rainy week. It doesn't rain too much in California, but when it does, it always seems to inspire me.

When it Rains

The water beats down
onto the pavement,
rolling off the rooftops,
washing away the world.
When it rains, the world goes quiet.
Nothing but the steady beat of the rain
against the window.
Nature's song
lulls me into comfort,
drowning out the real world
and quieting the storm
that rages in my own mind.
Standing out in the rain,
all of the stains that scar my innocence
are washed away.
I am cleansed, even if only for a moment.
The rain is intrusive,
powerful,
abrasive,
charismatic,
strong,
and most of all,
it's beautiful.

It Swirls

(Relationships)

Around You

Find people who
love to write and
hang out with them.

Incandescent

It started as a small feeling
It bubbled and frothed
And left me moments I was stealing
Ever changing, ever growing, effervescent

The sun set on the salty air
And I carry you into my soul
I take the leap, I take the dare
You seem to light that endless hole; ever incandescent

I am the fly, you are the light
You draw me in, but push me out
I go against the waves; push with all my might
Alive again; ever fluorescent.

Estella Gonzalez, mentor

I wrote this love poem at a WriteGirl In-Schools session where we used Elizabeth Barrett Browning's famous love sonnet as a template. In this case, it's a love poem one of my characters writes for her junior high school crush.

The Jorge Sonnet

How do I love my Jorge? Let me count all the crazy ways.
I love him so hard that I want to eat
him for breakfast like a plate of huevos rancheros.
I love him like a twenty-dollar bill, folded up tight into little square,
tucked in my back pocket.
I love him like one of those East L.A. dogs
chasing you as you peddle fast and desperate on your Huffy bike.
Without him, I am a dirty rose growing next to my dirty house.
Without him, I'm the lost soul
they teach you about in catechism, praying
in the middle of hell, stretching out chained arms.
I'll love him even after
he dumps me for the pimple-free girl,
just because people tell me not to.

Kate Johannesen, age 16

*I wrote this during a session with my mentor.
It was cold that day, and I was inspired by the color blue.*

Almost Blue

You are blushing
And your lips are
Almost blue
Our noses are touching
And this kiss is
Almost through

Your sweet laughter
Is lighter than air
It swirls around you
Surrounds you
Plays with your hair

And the light
Is just right

The world is wild
The world is still
And all is sound
And silence

Write about
how you feel and
what you want.

This was done during a session with my mentee, Majah Carberry.
The prompt was to write in the voice of a rope about to snap.

By a Thread

Hanging tightly
Hovering near the end of the earth
As frayed and as worn thin as
My patience
Heavy with responsibility
Brittle with fear
Red lights flashing on blind eyes
You hold me as
An anchor holds its vessel
But attached to the abyss
No lifeline
A paradox of conflicting answers as to why we fight
You beg for the truth
While you pray for lies
And the abyss stares back without
Saying hello
Until the fight seeps out of
My veins
And one becomes two

Rightful Place

Suddenly
Your world stopped
And with it, my desire
To seep into it, no more

Gone, halted
Never to be resurrected
No matter what miracle
Or pagan priest desired

You were translucent powder
Roaming the earth
You were the state of nothing
So casually claiming
Your rightful place in my life

Wendy Garcia, age 17

Until Midnight

I stay up until midnight
disappointed
that he did not show up.

I wait on the porch until midnight
disappointed
that I did not get that kiss.

Stars shine on me until midnight
disappointed
that he did not arrive.

I sleep until midnight,
and wake from my dream.
He did not forget about me.

Jessica Reben, age 18

Let You Go

Even though I'm in love,
I feel a little blue,
'cause I want this to work,
but I keep doubting myself.

I start to glow when I see you.
Thoughts of you
fill my mind every second.

I've never shed a tear,
never a frown on my face.
What is this?

What if I get boring?
What if you don't like me anymore?
What if you leave and I'm left alone?

I must back out.
Save you from me,
say good-bye,
get this feeling out of my body.

I might love you,
so you should know:
leave now,
before I let you go.

Something That Is True

I was sad that night
Fell asleep with swallowed tears
Jammed down my throat
The morning after, the sky was laced with moisture

You graced my day with light
Bringing warmth to all things
In the midst of lies
You are my truth

All too quickly the day returns to night
But in the faith of a first love, I find refuge
Blessed with something new
To grace the world

Don't be afraid
to use lines from an
email you wrote.
Sometimes our best
writing comes from an
unexpected place.

Berna Roberts, mentor

*This is based on the loss of my husband,
my healing process, and the ability to let go.*

The Beginning

You came and stole yourself from me
You stole yourself and hid in the sunrise
The sunrise that usually is the birth of a new day
A clean slate
First growth
New hope
A beginning that God has put upon us
The morning to start again
In the light of the dawn
Though it was not a beginning
But the beginning of an end
An unraveling from long ago that bore no witness
No resolution
No savior
A bird whose broken wings had finally healed
And it was time
Time to fly away
In the light of the day

Andrea Lopez, age 17

I wrote this because I have someone very special to me who lives far away.

Across the World

From the endless night sky to the ocean of stars,
within a flash, our worlds collide.
Take my hand and we'll go
where we belong.

We will be free
like birds flying across the deep blue sea,
together throughout the journey.

What kind of love is this?
We have states, countries and an ocean separating us,
but it's only so long until you'll be here, next to me.

Know that when you stare out into the night sky,
with the moon shining upon you,
I'm on the other side, staring back at you,
wishing you were here with me, too.

Brittany Delva, 14

This was written at the WriteGirl Songwriting Workshop.

Me and LaCarrie

LaCarrie, when you went away
I was so lonely, remembering the day
We danced outside in the rain
Felt the sun warming our skin

It felt so right, the times we'd fight
Now I'm lost in this sorrow tonight
I even miss when we cried in pain
When I think of you, I say your name
LaCarrie

The last time I saw your beautiful face
You left me feeling so out of place
I felt as if I'd lost a part of me
Memories so so tender and sweet

It felt so right, the times we'd fight
Now I'm lost in this sorrow tonight
I even miss when we cried in pain
When I think of you, I say your name
LaCarrie

Zoe Isabella Camp, age 15

*A friend of mine was going through a rough time
and asked me what I thought love was.*

Love

Love is hell
death
something you never want to be involved in –
a murderous weapon used to destroy the hearts of every victim.
Love is poison.
Love is you.
Love is the happiness you gave me
and the pain that has taken its place.
The dreams I had of us being together
and the nightmares that haunt my sleep.
Love is seeing you in the halls and my heart skipping a beat,
wishing I never met you.
Love is pain, suffering,
a disease that follows you and destroys your life.
Love is wishing I could cut out our memories
and throw them into the ocean.
Love is a silence my life has been brought to
because of you.
Love is pain, poison.
Love is you.

Linda Alonzo, age 17

Sometimes déjà vu feels like a dream.
I had this dream two years ago.

Déjà Vu

Tick…tick…tick…tick… The clocks tick very loud. I don't know the time, but it must be very late. At some point I fall asleep. I dream of a boy. He is sitting across from me, his face in his hands. I can hear him crying and I stare at him until he finally notices that I am watching him. He looks around and starts to sob harder.

"Hey guy, what's wrong? Why are you crying?"

He looks straight at me, but he cannot see me. I start to get frustrated. It is as though I am looking at him through a window. I feel horrible; I want to get out of the room and comfort this stranger.

I see a girl walking. She is heading straight for him. She is shorter than me and skinnier. Her hair is long, past her shoulders. She gets in my way and tells the boy something. He starts to sob once more.

The window shatters. I jump back to avoid the broken glass. That's when I wake up.

Tick…tick…tick…tick. I remember little childhood memories. At school, I keep getting distracted, looking out the window, wondering if it will shatter and lead me into a world of fantasies.

Darren, my best friend, keeps poking me with his pencil. He knows something is bothering me. I met Darren in my dreams when I was small. In my dreams, he looked like he does now – tall, scrawny, curly hair and glasses. I thought he was just a dream; never thought of him being someone real.

When I started here at Vancouver High, I had mostly forgotten about him. When we saw each other, we both just stared and kept walking. He existed. Strange, but completely familiar.

Write when you are so mad that you feel like you are going to burst.

Lullaby Dreams of Him

I wanted to love him in such a way that no one would notice the heart muscle that pulsated a little too rapidly, or the speech that was nervous. I wanted to shove all that down to the basement of my psyche, to the overpriced storage closet that doesn't get opened.

I wanted to choke the words that were begging to leap from my tongue like a goldfish on a suicidal jump out of its glass bowl. There was no rational reason to release a heart that had been methodically covered with protective gauze that stopped the generous bleeding of an old wound.

I wanted to love him in a way that would keep the protective layers intact, so I wouldn't have to unbundle years of winter preparation. To de-layer means you aren't protected from the next emotional tide. It's easier to maintain a close watch on all feelings. Early detection is best. Find the feeling. Identify it. Kill it.

Some people eschew the obvious route to your heart. With each chuckle, each revelation of an intimate secret, they take their time unbandaging you, until one afternoon, when I realized there was a slight shift beneath me. The earth moved long enough to allow a crack of light to shine through the floor.

He came into my life, sweet like jelly beans and candy-coated dimples. He was a world of bear hugs and saccharine grins. Lullaby thoughts of him in my sleep. The ticking train schedule of my life placed on hold. My heart's temperature rising. Desiring to capture his lightning bug in my jar before summer was over.

Rebecca Leff, age 17

Time

Heavens roar
And fires ice
The blue across the sky
In painful streaks of blood and hope
The time she tries to hide

A ticking hand
Beats down like rain
In chains of a lover's embrace
The stagnant kiss of music's quiet
Tears rafting down her face

Time holds
It cracks
It never understands
It knows what humans feel
As the heavens hold back
A hellish laugh
And the wounds just begin to heal

Tracy DeBrincat, mentor

This was written during a mentoring session where we used a childhood memory to generate a fictional text.

Running Down Beech Street in a Blue Nightgown

The dog trots just fast enough to stay out of my reach.
His ears blow back in the wind. His tongue lolls. He smiles.
Each tree, each lamppost, each bush belongs to him.
I have a stitch in my side from running.
The concrete is cold on my feet.

The sky hangs over me, gray and wet,
reminding me of the dog's lack of a name,
my inability to keep him on a leash,
to teach him to come when called,
sit when told, or lie quietly at my feet beside a roaring fire.

The roaring fire is all in my head.
Let the dog go, I think. He'll be better off without me.
Let someone else groom, walk and feed him,
gather his two-toned hair from their clothes,
neutralize his musty smell.

My bones rattle as I turn toward home, but I grimace and savor the chill.
The dog is waiting at the gate when I arrive,
pushes past me when I open the door.
It is not often I get to feel this much all at one time.
I think I will name him Jerome.

Hadley Dion, age 16

I wrote this piece at WriteGirl Welcome Day at a writing station called "Snapshot Stories," where we were asked to write a piece of fiction based on a photograph.

A Waltz Frozen in Time

"Dance with me," he whispered, as he took her weathered hand into his own. He thought to himself that she had never looked more beautiful. The curls of her snowy hair framed her delicate jaw and her ruby red lips enriched her ivory complexion.

They waltzed gracefully past a line of freshly hung laundry. He twirled her and Lila remembered the first time they danced – a moment suspended when her eyes met his, warm and blue, and they conquered the dance floor. A car alarm sounded and dogs barked in the distance – the symphony of urban Los Angeles. All they heard were their footsteps in the damp grass.

Endless years had passed, with doors slammed and nights spent on the couch, daily walks and rants over lost socks, gossip about neighbors and sweet jazz music on the ancient record player, but there were still butterflies when their cheeks touched. They recognized their existence in the hearts that beat inches away.

Sometimes they wondered how they would cope without the other. They worried about the days to come. A widowed future had occupied their minds more than once. But in this moment, hand-in-hand and cheek-to-cheek, worry would not dare come out to play.

You'll never know
what works for you
unless you try
something new.

Karina Sanchez, age 17

Strong

I sit still, then move onto my knees. I intertwine my hands and place them under my chin. I close my eyes, hoping this will bring me closer to Buddha. I try to pray but large tears start to roll down my cheeks. I cry for my forbidden love, for the problems and shame I have brought to my family, but most of all, I cry for me.

I'm in love with Eli, but we can't be together, for I am a Hindu and he's a Jew and we can't change who we are. We once considered running away. It would be just the two of us: Eli and Irene. But we knew we'd be sad to leave our families behind. As I pray to Buddha, I ask for strength because today I must tell Eli good-bye.

I also pray for Eli. I want him to be happy and even though it hurts to think about it, I hope he finds someone else to...

I can't finish the thought. The pain in my chest feels like my heart is literally breaking. I will never love anyone else like Eli, but I will be strong. I will continue with my life and Eli with his. I will marry a Hindu and my family will be happy.

I take a deep breath and one last time, I ask Buddha to give me strength.

Jennifer Ayuso, age 16

This is about a prophecy that took countless hours of dreaming and a Poetry Workshop at WriteGirl.

Solace (an excerpt)

In a time of lovers, time is irrelevant – yet always cut short. I walk steadily, hands clutched into fists, holding my feelings, and no air passes by these demons. Wishing not to feel now, I arise from my slumber. No wandering soul should know my name (for any who have will soon learn to regret it). I reached the point where I thought everything was nothing…and yet nothing…was everything. Suddenly, just hearing your voice guides me through the pitch darkness; the sweet-sounding, soothing ray of light that eases all my doubts and fears. My solace.

(Portraits)

Crooked Jaw

Take a cliché
and turn it
on its head.

Menudo

I know this girl. Her name
is Joanna, Mexican-Honduran
Beauty Queen, mother of one at fourteen
I know this girl. She made me *chorizos*,
she introduced me to my first *pupusa*,
she was the first girl I kissed.
I know her; she's walking up right now
in a skin-tight black V-neck, skinny jeans
and Vans, eyeliner, a precise silhouette of her
top lid. I know Iris, palms sweaty,
hair crinkled with Aquanet hairspray and mousse.
I know *mi hermana*, my tan sister, a subdued,
superb shade of brown. I know Coralia, she
has *Jose* tattooed on her neck, her Baby Daddy, her love.
I know Barbie/Eeyore/Droopy/Blanca/Flaca/
Skittles, I know how R's roll off her tongue,
I know the sound of one-dollar rosaries
hitting her chest, I know the click clack
clang bang of her silver hoops, I know her.
She is my best friend; she is my childhood confidante.
She is old news, new tears.
Forgotten girl, formed by corroding,
rooftops, infantile screams,
menudo and premature motherhood.

*Know what your character wants.

Victoria

Victoria was a hardworking girl who wanted to become a dancer. She worked at El Balcón, a small bistro restaurant. Every day she served and waited on tables diligently, hoping that one day she could dance onstage. Then, while she was waiting on an order, one of the main dancers broke her leg. She was finally going to have her dream come true! But there was one problem – the manager wanted a new pair of dancers. She needed to find the perfect man, but she couldn't think of anyone.

One night, when it was her day to close the restaurant, she stayed to practice onstage. She put on one of the dancer's costumes and pulled up her hair. She danced and danced and was about to press play for one last dance when the manager came in. She froze, afraid she had ruined all her chances of becoming a dancer at El Balcón.

This Indian Woman

This Indian woman is overwhelmed
By the power of her god
She prays and never gets
What she is asking for

Her mother died
And she wants her back
Her father is ill
He is all she has

She prays
With all her heart
In the same exact spot
Every single day

She prays so hard
And nothing happens
Except a rich young man
Asking for her hand

This man is a prince
If she doesn't accept
She is missing her chance
Of being his wife

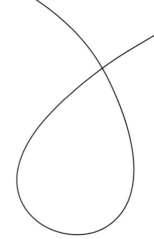

If she accepts
She must leave her father
She does not know what to do
So she asks for more time

Her father says go
She doesn't need him anymore
She wants to stay
Out of love

In the end she marries the god
And cries whenever she prays
Now her prayers are sincere
They come from her heart

DO:
Leave a piece of writing alone for a while

Don't:
Leave a story unfinished!

Samantha Skelton, age 17

Evol, the main character in this short story, is feeling overwhelmed.

Run (an excerpt)

The morning is frigid, wintry, and I'm on a run. My lungs are wheezing. My thighs burn like flames, but I need to get it out of me. I have to forget what I heard on the news that night.

I run hard, fueled by my misery. I feel like I'm about to be in a boxing match.

Snow surrounds me. The ice-cold landscape is in tune with my heart. I sprint as fast as I can around the frozen lake.

I'm so confused and angry these days. Running is the only thing I know how to do without torturing myself. I breathe harder, harder, faster, faster. My hot breath fills the air like smoke rising.

I feel a tear slowly roll down my cheek, and a memory crystallizes: I'm on this same run, only my whole life is different.

McKenzie Givens, age 15

This piece was written during a mentoring session at a restaurant in Venice Beach. The subject of the poem, one of many strange characters native to Venice, lingered for only a moment in the window.

Midday Music

Perfect concentration
in a blue-framed tableau.
Hand-rolled cigarettes,
made the way father taught.

Metallic memories of wartime,
love & loss hover over heartbeats.
A leather jacket creased
by countless arm-raisings (in triumph and surrender).

With crooked jaw and cavernous cheeks,
he is the master of a solitary kingdom.
Caught in an eternally-looping mind-film,
dark figure of the dying age (downcast eyes, hunched shoulders).

The last youthful attempt at resistance
fades as the cherry red lighter is pocketed.
Without notice, the screen begins to flicker
and the image fades.

Lexy Folkes, age 18

*This piece was written during a WriteGirl workshop.
The prompt was, "What makes you feel powerful?"
Some moments in life are almost indescribable,
but, when you can find the right words to
capture them, that in itself is empowering.*

Prime Time

It is 4 a.m. The sound of the alarm taunts her in her dream, until she realizes
it is her signal to wake. Normally, she hits the snooze button hard enough
to make sure the thing never cries again. Today is different; this is a
premeditated act of inspiration. She selects her clothing from the piles she
laid out the night before. She is dressed in workout clothes, running shoes and,
as always, mismatched socks. Everyone knows matching socks are bad luck.

The freeway cannot keep up with her as the gas pedal flirts with the floor
of her car. The sun still sleeps under a blanket of morning twilight. The long
drive from her sleeping city to the sandy shores seems short, as adrenaline
fuels her.

She comes upon the first sight of the beach and is infused with a surge of
power. She has arrived. She gets out of the car and slams the door. She runs
from the parking lot to the cold, wet sand and takes off sprinting. A smile
cracks across her face as she looks down at her shoes straining against the
sand, leaving a puckered path of footprints behind her. She has won. She has
beaten the sun.

The seagulls' timely cries signal the sun's awakening. It yawns behind her,
pulling off its twilight blanket as it casts rays of dim light across the shore.
This is it. This is life at its prime. The air tastes of salt and victory.

Reparata Mazzola, mentor

Technology was stressing me out,
so I vented in this piece!

My Smart Phone

My smart phone needs an IQ test. As soon as I could afford a data package, I bought one of those Einstein communicators. I was so *au courant*. While I enjoy instant Googling to confront smart alecks who don't have their facts right, or finding obscure information like how flies mate, the phone has its dumb moments. When I check my call log, I have apparently dialed numbers with bizarre area codes. Calling back gets me a Verizon message that the number is no longer in service. Apparently, I now also have special powers: I can dial without ever touching the phone. While we're watching TV, my boyfriend asks, "Why are you calling me?" The phone is three feet away! And the voice dialer has been possessed. It sometimes commands, "Speak now," and without my speaking, dials some random number. Of course, there's the all-popular 'pocket dial.' So often, my friends ring and say, "Did you just call me?" I didn't but we get to have a nice long chat!

Can I go back to my old flip phone? No way. So, I'll keep googling and navigating and downloading apps until the cows come home...good thing they don't have GPS!

Taylor Norris, age 18

This piece was written during one of my writing sessions with my mentor. She wanted me to try something new, something that did not concern boys or love.

Intensity

Cold winter day; the air is crisp. Leaves blow gently, rustling. A small rock sits in a pile of dirt like a person lost in a crowd. It has a shine, yet it is not perfect. It longs to get out and experience the world, like a baby who is trying to crawl. Advancing. Becoming more than what is expected. A small rock trying to make it in a big world.

A boy sees the rock, sees something special, picks it up. He cleans the rock as if it were a medal, shining it as a proud athlete would. He places it in his pocket and takes it on a trip.

In Chicago, Illinois, the boy takes this rock and drops it from the top of a 50-story building. As the rock falls, tumbling through the air gracefully like a dancer floating across the stage, it believes this is its time to shine.

It lands in water with a huge splash. But is this water? Or merely a dream? The water it imagined it has landed in isn't water. The rock realizes that the fame it so longed for isn't the kind of fame it desires. It has killed a man.

The boy set it up; and now it will be known as "The Rock that Killed the Governor of Illinois." Sometimes our dreams don't turn out as planned.

Karen Toledo, age 18

My literature teacher gave me a lovely printed picture of a huge black beast, and what caught most of my attention was its marvelously crafted face.

My Best Fiend

Black beast, snarling grin
Greets the world outside your window

Your canines stab
Like sinister stalactites
Guarding an ancient cave roof

Your lolling tongue
Hangs out like a carpet
Holding your heavy breath

Black beast, serpent eyes
Target whatever is outside your window

Your glare is predatory
Filled with intensity
But you are made of meat, too

From afar you rival the devil's pet
Cerberus, but too soft to the touch
Fine furry locks in the spotlight of the sun

Black beast, your glow
Greets the world outside your window

Read!

Read for knowledge and inspiration.

Cactus Man

He is an ugly man
In a prickly suit
His romances short and painful
His shoulders broad and wide

He considers himself a survivalist
His food is his punishment
His diamonds so unkind –
Thus his lovers are so scarce

He lives in fear
One day the porcelain
So dry in his grasp
Might crack beneath him

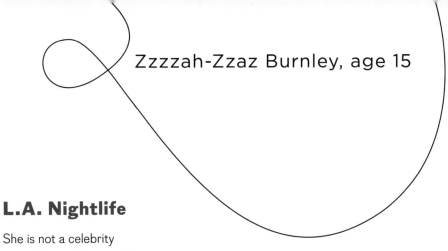

Zzzzah-Zzaz Burnley, age 15

L.A. Nightlife

She is not a celebrity
spends late nights in clubs
making observations
giving critiques
getting paid for
who she is.

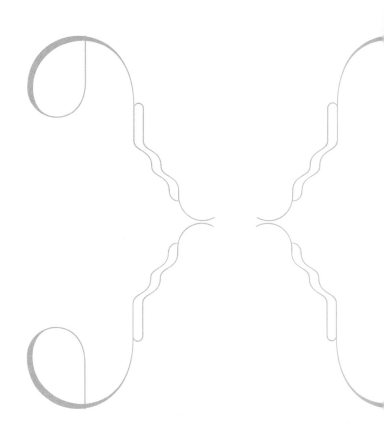

A Soldier's Pain

As I close my eyes, he is
Haunting me now all over again
I hear his gurgle and each gasp for breath
In the quiet darkness

His memory is poison to my body
Lips dry, pale, chapped and ghostly white
I cringe as he stares at me with those eyes
Am I awake or am I just dreaming?

I've forgotten who I am and gone mad
Tired of being haunted by this man
Torn by actions I can never fix
Guilty inside, a soldier always is

Tiny Dancer

She walks like the tiny dancer she is.
Make way for her bruised, colored toes.
She's looking for someone to hold her.
"Hold me closer, Tiny Dancer."

She's worked through blood and body image to get here.
Our teacher could see the hard talent from the very beginning.
She was going to be a hardworking ballerina someday.

I can't imagine how her little sugar plum fairy toes *pas de bourrée*
on broken feet toward another act.
I know she's worked hard for this,
and I know how hard it was for her to keep that image –
to look like a ballerina.

Austin, Texas, please let her in.
Her tear-stained eyes can't look in the mirror anymore.
She's stared for too long and too critically at her own body.
She's worked hard –
this Tiny Dancer has worked the hardest.

GALAXY OF WORDS

(WRITING)

Write bold and write proud because nothing you have to say is over the top.

Sarah Villegas, age 16

My mentor asked me to try and write a poem to my favorite poet.
I do not have a favorite, so I just wrote it to the first poet I knew, my dad.

Poet

Hidden from me for decades of words
Not ashamed, but patient
The star in your galaxy showed you
I could shine bright
In revealing thunderous poetry

An awkward moment
Vague, beautiful words mended together
You spoke softly, with hidden urge
Not to scare the deer into its twilight forest
But to draw it near to vast meadows of grain and lavender

Under beaming sunlight,
You drew me into the beauty of writing
I came willingly, nibbling at herbs and berries
Techniques and methods
To express oneself

My own meadow, planted now
Will continue to grow
But I will still wander
Into your serene meadow,
Initial place of my free spirit

Glenda L. Richardson, mentor

This was inspired after seeing my friend's one-woman show,
"The Last Torn Page."

Word Play

I play with their words endlessly, toiling to make them fit on one page instead
of two, working with them like mathematics to come to their very safe one
answer instead of all the more colorful answers that could be.

And I struggle to remember my voice in this city of lost angels
fighting the words I truly crave to write
for the words they make me write
because I am invisible
and in order to be visible
you need to be respected
and in order to be respected, you must pay your dues.
Or do you?

These words used to have a sweetness to them,
honest and bold;
and they'd roll off my fingertips like melted butter.
Now there is only this longing, a deep-seated desire for what is not
and contempt and frustration for what is.
They are still mine, yes,
but they come from a different place
and I yearn for that other place
where I used to be.

In one of my weekly mentoring sessions, my mentor
suggested that we both write about why we write.

Why I Write

I want to feel. I want to be able to see life with clarity, and I want to understand why we are all so different. In order to keep absorbing, I must write to discover what I need to hold on to and what I need to let go of.

Writing is like cleaning out a closet. Whenever I am feeling filled to the brim, when emotions and current battles fill my pockets and my body, it is my time to write. Putting pen to paper lets me tell the story that I am not ready for people to hear me say out loud. I listen to the world around me and process the pain and the goodness that I find. Allowing myself to stop, think, and write gives me the opportunity to react and form my own opinions. Without such an outlet, every occurrence in my life could only ever be received with more and more numbness.

Sometimes it is best to get rid of an old pair of jeans to make room for something better. Sometimes I need to get it all out so that I can see what is really important. Writing is a cleaning, a clarifying, and a healing process.

Yasmine Alfakey, age 17

Chronic Writer's Block

Dear readers, listeners, family and friends,
I would like to blame this incident
on my pen.
With an empty hollow tube in my hand,
how could I possibly write again?
Surely I have thoughts in mind –
a world of literature stored behind my eyes.
But what more can I say
if my pen simply won't write more today?
Maybe I'll text you a line or two.
There must be something I can do.
But I won't; I must have forgotten –
my phone, too, has become rotten.

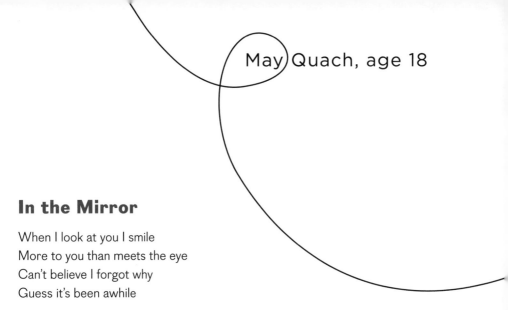

May Quach, age 18

In the Mirror

When I look at you I smile
More to you than meets the eye
Can't believe I forgot why
Guess it's been awhile

When I look I at you I review
To see how I appear
With all your hopes and fears
The reflection of me in you

Anissa Johnson, mentor

Stream of Consciousness

12:01 PM

I stroll into my favorite neighborhood coffee shop. The owner, an elderly woman with silver hair, a flower print polyester dress and black orthopedic shoes watches me, eerily daring me to think I can write in her establishment without purchasing a cup of day-old coffee masquerading as freshly brewed. Calming my inner rebel and acknowledging my respect for the elderly, I settle on a cup of herbal tea. She rings me up and I take a seat in my favorite corner, next to my favorite window, in my favorite love seat, cuddled to my favorite fluffed pillow. I try not to think where it's been.

12:10 PM

I search my computer screen for words that aren't there. I wait for literary genius, but instead feel the inspiration of Dr. Seuss. *The Cat in the Hat* stanzas rotate in my head like spinning wheels. My chest tightens at the betrayal.

12:25 PM

The clanging of glasses, the roaring of espresso machines, restless chatter, the soft jingle of a bell as doors open and close. Three teenage girls have conversations about the new boy in school, warring mothers and abandoned sidekicks. The clock is ticking, but for now I'll daydream.

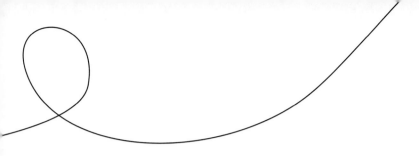

12:45 PM

I realize I'm getting nothing done. My thoughts are scattered like wind blowing through tossed trash left out by my neighbor, the cute neighbor. I go to his Facebook page and rifle through his photos, envision myself holding the camera as if he were sharing the most intimate details of his life with only me...nightmares of a day wasted...get yourself together.

1:00 PM

I take a look at an empty Word doc, pray for focus and begin typing. Surprisingly, the words now come easily, the letters spread across my computer screen like water swallowing sand dunes.

Cut whatever
is not working.
Be _brave._

Jacqueline Wilson, mentor

Like most writers, every time I sit down to write, I struggle with feelings of insecurity and end up with "writer's block;" but it's so important to face those feelings, and to write in spite of them.

The Blank Page

It stared at her with an accusing glare, like her mother did when she was sixteen and failed to do her weekly chores. It was a silent, passive-aggressive, "You know what you did and I don't have to say a word" glare. She *hated* that glare.

It happened every time she sat down to write. She'd sit there with her armor on, determined but inevitably drawing a blank. It was *just* a page, gosh darn it, a simple rectangle on her computer screen, egg-white in its innocence. But it taunted her.

"Are you really a writer?" it asked. Then had the nerve to demand that she fill it with words, words that would shape themselves into unforgettable characters and dialogue; words that would win her accolades and shiny gold statues; words that would *change the world!* The pressure was driving her nuts.

Suddenly, the bathroom she'd cleaned two days ago needed another once over. Hey! Her best friend Chris is calling from New York – that'll kill three hours. Wait! Let's watch every *Buffy the Vampire Slayer* DVD for the ninth time! That'll create some inspiration!

But the page continued to haunt her, even from the confines of a powered-down laptop. It would not be denied its pound of flesh. So she sat down, pried open the jaws of the beast – uh, her laptop – and faced the endless emptiness.

Then something happened: a thought popped into her head. Then another one, and soon words were fighting for space on the page. She had no idea if they would win her shiny gold statues, but she was *writing* and that was all that mattered.

(Writing Experiments)

Sing Your Word Song

WRITING EXPERIMENT:

Take a line of writing from anywhere — a book, a poster, the back of a shampoo bottle, the tag on a stuffed animal. Use that line as the first line of your poem. Go!

Kimberly Fero, mentor

I wrote this during the WriteGirl Poetry Workshop. My mentee and I were challenged to write a poem starting with the line, "The people I love the best," from Marge Piercy's poem, "To Be of Use." We loved how much we learned about each other just by sharing these short pieces.

I'm Not Here to Save the World

The people I love the best
are the humble, simple, everyday
sort of ordinary.

Rich with human flaws, they muddle
through the day-to-day
like elephants

tiptoeing through a field
of
flattened
daisies.

Lisa Beebe, mentor

I wrote this at WriteGirl's Poetry Workshop, from a writing prompt inspired by Marge Piercy's poem, "To Be of Use," which shares the same first line.

My People

The people I love the best
Do not care if their hair
Falls out of place.

They leap on trampolines,
Bouncing free of gravity,
Squealing with laughter,
Daring the earth to reel them back in.

Their umbrellas go unused
Because raindrops tickle,
And an umbrella-free hand
Can rescue wayward snails.

My people wear color.
They sparkle!
(Whether or not sparkle's trendy)

They smile so big their eyes wrinkle up
And they tag those photos with pride.

My people remind me to stop working
On a perfect L.A. day.
My people always
make time to play.

Rich language
is eye candy to
the reader.
Spice it up!

Emily Carroll, mentor

People I Love the Best

The people I love the best
Share themselves like a delicate flower,
No charades or gimmicks
Because they know the complex texture
At the core of their being
Is revealing, beautiful and dramatic enough,
The colors of an intricate pastel sunset.

WRITING EXPERIMENT:

A building can be inspiration for writing. Take a walk and see what buildings speak to you.

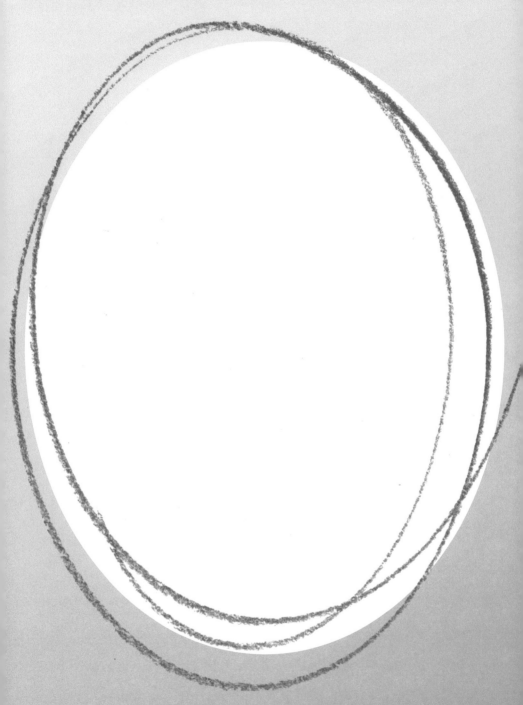

Write first.
Edit later.

Arlene Granadosin, mentor

I wrote this at the WriteGirl Poetry Workshop during the segment led by Xochitl-Julisa Bermejo. It is a poem inspired by the Victor Clothing Company building in Los Angeles, CA.

Blue Sentinel

Blue groom with his cummerbund
And ruffled shirt
Standing sentinel over his
Beautiful web-haired
Bride
He leans, chest out, to signal
I am here; we are here
We are each other's
And our togetherness can
Be eternal
He is a guard
A self-appointed soldier of
His sweetheart's
Solitude
Stoic and solemn

WRITING EXPERIMENT:

Try a new form, such as haiku, sonnet, ghazal or villanelle.
Form can give your writing an inner strength.

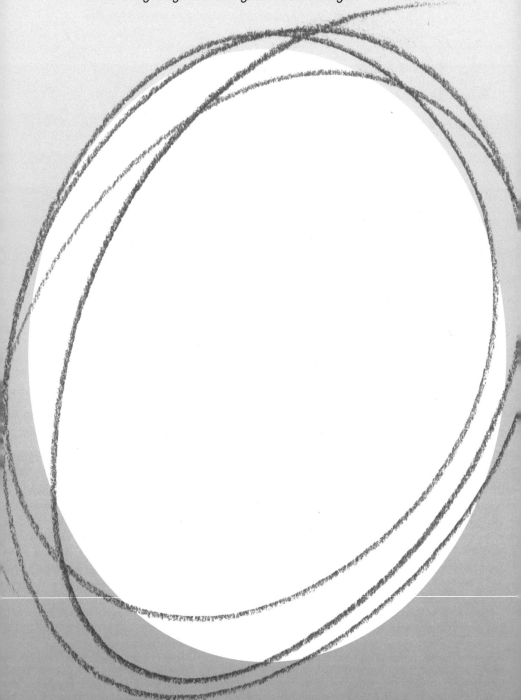

Katherine Thompson, mentor

I love experimenting with form in poetry, and villanelles are the most difficult ones I've ever tried. I wrote this one for a dear friend and mentor, thinking about how everything is temporary.

Villanelle for Lucy

Your world is the tapestry you weave
with words, with love, with patience even when
you are painting a house you are about to leave.

Mountains may migrate, memories deceive,
cities can crumble, but you do not weaken.
Your world is the tapestry you weave.

Once, you wiped a tear upon your sleeve,
took up a brush, dipped it in the tin,
and painted a house you were about to leave.

Each brushstroke bled beauty, made you grieve
for your homesick heart, this empty room in
your world. Is the tapestry you weave

a figment of faith, or something to believe?
In life, there is no comparable compassion
to painting a house you are about to leave,

to letting its new inhabitants conceive
the home waiting to sprout within.
Our world is made of tapestries we weave
while painting the house we are about to leave.

Read your writing back to yourself out loud.

WRITING EXPERIMENT:

Take a poem. Read it forward and backward. Get inside of the poem. Hear its rhythm, its pulse, feel its meaning. Then write your own poem in the same vein or spirit.

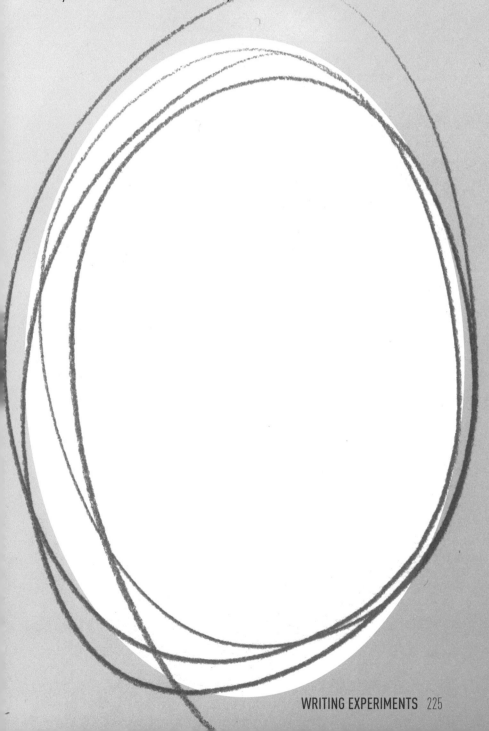

Annie Brown, mentor

I wrote this piece in a sunny, crowded café with my mentee Jillian, using a poem by William Carlos Williams as a model.

An Homage to William Carlos Williams

This is just to say
I've eavesdropped
from across the café
on your conversation
which you might have wanted
kept in confidence.

Forgive me,
your gossip was
so loud
and so juicy.

Love the fact that you are able to do such a wonderful thing—write.

Amber Caron, mentor

This poem was inspired by Anne Sexton's
"For John, Who Begs Me Not to Enquire Further."

For My First Grade Teacher Mrs. Brown, Who Begged Me to Stay in the Lines

Not that it was beautiful, but the lines were thin,
the numbers were small, the code was confusing.
And in the end, there was a certain beauty in the way
the purple mixed with the brown,
the way the bear balanced not just the ball with its narrow stripes,
but also the purple heart and my name
on its nose.

And if I tried to give you something else
inside the lines,
then you would not know
that it isn't the worst for any artist
to color a two
purple instead of blue.
You paced behind me,
and I tapped my green crayon;
the tip was flat and the glossy wrapper
wrinkled under the pressure.
I peeled the skin away and the green wax
mixed with the dirt under my fingernail.
You sighed as you watched me color his eyes green.
It is a small thing to rage with a green crayon.

And if you turn it down,
leave it on the circular table at the back of the room
while you hang the others on the wall,
I will hold my bear,
with all its patches of color,
and write a new world around it,
as if I were telling his life to the boy next to me
whose brown bear
has nothing to help,
no name to support,
and no words to act as a cage,
so that it might just walk off his page.

Show up.
Have fun!

WRITING EXPERIMENT:

Find a photo in your home, at a flea market, in a newspaper or in your mail. Spend some time with it, notice all the details. Get lost in it. Then start writing. Write about what you see or write about what you don't see. Write what might happen next, or write from the perspective of one of the characters or objects in the photo.

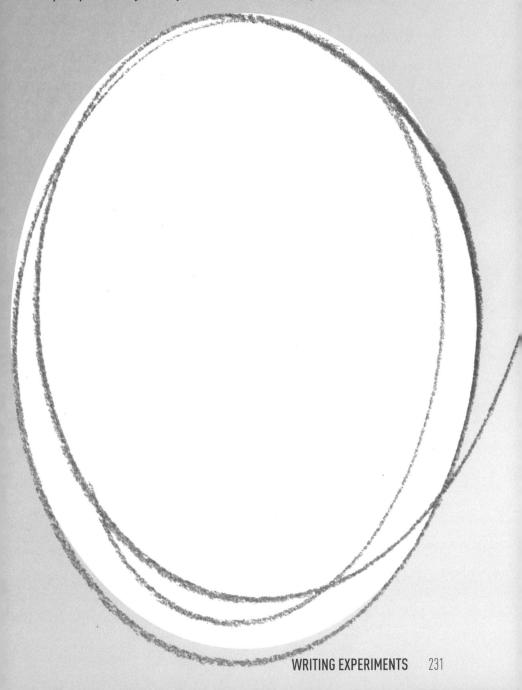

Rachel Burdorf, age 14

I wrote this piece at the WriteGirl Poetry Workshop when a guest speaker brought in pictures of murals from all over L.A. and asked us to write a poem. I chose a picture of a couple, several stories tall, probably at their wedding. Neither of them looked happy and the entire thing was in shades of blue.

Two Dimensions

As I stare out of my faded wall, I see everything: people bundled against the cold, cars, birds, clouds, sorrows, the occasional stray dog interspersed with brief snatches of conversation on the wind, all coming and going.

One person sits cross-legged on the cracked sidewalk, seemingly oblivious to the morning chill. She does not come or go. Instead, she hugs her jacket as the wind whips the small strands of hair that escape her hood. Small pieces of trash cartwheel by, a plastic bag and granola bar wrapper, but she does not notice.

My frozen, painted eyes meet her blinking, squinting ones, and I wonder what's going through her mind.

> *I sit on the worn sidewalk, hunched to conserve the heat, grasping my jacket with chilled fingers. As the cold seeps up through the ground, its fingers brushing my legs, I stare up at the mural on the wall in front of me.*
>
> *The woman's two-story face stares out at me bitterly: her shoulders set, her head held high, a question in her painted eyes.*
>
> *As the wind tosses my hair and stings my eyes, I stare back and I wonder: What's going through her mind?*

Inez Singletary, mentor

*Written at a WriteGirl workshop, inspired by a picture of a mural
of a Madonna who was light and dark, a blue shadow with light
breaking on one side of her face. She wore a stained glass corona.*

Blue Madonna

Singing with her eyes closed
And her mouth closed, too.
In her heart, she sings, and I hear.
Soft and powerful, her blessing resounds
Throughout the city halls, homes, highways and walls.
She sings her blessing, eyes closed, open inside.
Yes, she sings.
Yes, you are beautiful little girl, little girl,
Pretty like my stain-colored corona,
Sacred and sweet you are.
Go, little girl!
Go full of rainbow.
Sing your word song.

Majah Carberry, age 16

We looked at various pictures of murals from around Los Angeles and described them.

Mural

Here we are. Take a picture.
His city lies before the eyes of an artist.
There's the scene of you,
sitting where you may, on a mountain
or in a dusty blue tow truck.
A square lens snaps the mind
on back alley concrete, where his
darkened hands hold thought
from any mile.
Where are you going? Let me out.
Unlock the caged glass and bricks.
The iron bars that pin him to
a story of velvet.
Here there is no desperation,
here there is the calm gaze
into the eyes of a criminal
or a betrayed loveline.
I'm staring from across the world,
from another space.
Here we see the magicality
of time travel, from which
dead voices speak silently
and blue eyes see only old decades.

Imani Crenshaw, age 17

I felt a need to tell the story of the characters in a blue Chicano mural in L.A.

Chicana Falsa

I love to sing and dance. Can't you tell? My toes tingle as I stand here every day! Love? *Mi amor*? Oh, he's here right next to me. He's blue right now; actually, he's blue every day. He stands here, doesn't say much but loves me every day. It's quite convenient, actually. A man who can love you without words. I'm a small part of Los Angeles, of togetherness, of you, *y tú*!

Emily Richmond, mentor

I don't tend to write poetry, but I wrote this at the WriteGirl Poetry Workshop. It was inspired by a picture of a woman standing squarely in front of a glorious mural painted on the side of a large building. The woman was looking through her purse or down at her feet.

Stopped

Standing small against the wall.
Head down, not up.
Hurried.
Taking a moment to stop moving,
But not stopping to be moved by the moment.

Corine Taylor, age 17

Hollywood Mural

A wide bun,
arched eyebrows
glancing down,
watching the people pass below her,
reflecting.
Warm swirls surround her,
memories escape through her ears,
encrypted messages outline her soul.
She watches the people of the city
pass below her
and she remains there –
trapped on a brick wall.

(Excerpted from our Creative Writing guide, *Pens on Fire: Creative Writing Experiments for Teens* from WriteGirl)

Screenwriting

Fish Out of Water
Think of a wacky or funny friend you have. Now imagine placing that friend in the exact OPPOSITE setting than that to which he or she is accustomed. (The movie term for this is "fish out of water.") Write a scene in which your friend has to interact with someone he or she would never normally talk to.

What I Wish I'd Said Was...
Go back to a moment in your life where you wish you'd said something different than what you actually did. Write a scene in which the perfect words come out of your mouth...satisfaction at last!

Creative Nonfiction

How to Make Me Happy
Write how someone can make you happy in three steps. Be specific – spell out exactly what kind of chocolate you want or what you would want this person to do for you.

Mix N' Match
Think about two interests that might not normally go together, and then put them together! Should the local gym have an all-you-can-eat buffet? What would it be like for Adopt-A-Pet to team up with an online dating service?

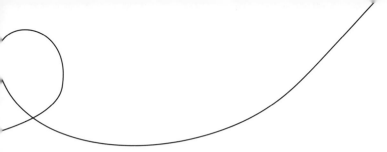

Poetry

Sometimes, Freedom Can Come from Restriction
Give yourself word limits. For example, write a poem about the last time you laughed or cried, using only five words per line. Explore words that bring depth to your poem.

I Am
Define yourself, in a poem. Declare how you see yourself, right here, right now.

Journalism

Pet Peeves
Make a list of things you don't like in your house and write an editorial about the things that frustrate you about your living situation. Try to keep the tone and style consistent, whether it's comedic, dramatic, or irritated. Be specific: early curfew, noisy brothers and sisters, no television.

Don't See This Movie…Or Do
Choose a movie, TV show, CD, or book and review it. Be careful not to give the whole thing away! Tell your readers why they should snatch it up, avoid it, or give it a shot if they have nothing better to do.

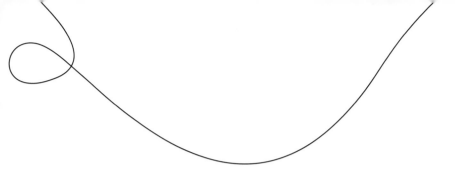

Fiction

Who's Your Muse?

In Greek mythology, there are four muses who inspire poets. Create a muse for yourself. Describe him or her – clothes, personality, special powers, the advice and inspiration your muse would impart.

Your Mother Likes Him but You Don't

After you've written a description of a character, describe this character again from the point of view of a different character. Think about specific mannerisms that drive you crazy: chewing gum with an open mouth, talking on a cell phone while ordering food, tapping fingers on a counter.

Songwriting

Change the Lyrics

Think of a song you know well. In your mind or out loud, listen to the melody to that song with "la la"s instead of the lyrics. Now replace the "la la"s with your own words.

What's in a Title?

Sometimes all you need to start writing is a great title. Look at the songs on a CD you don't know. Pick one of the titles and write your own song. After you're done, listen to the original.

Journal Writing

Dear Prudence
Start off a journal entry with "Dear Somebody." You choose. It can be somebody fictional or real.

Smell It
The sense of smell is the most powerful sense to evoke memories. Think of one smell, the first that pops into your head, and write about a memory that goes with it.

Essay

Inspiration
Write about a relative, teacher or friend who has influenced you the most and why. Focus on a specific way that person that shaped who you are today.

The World Today
What is the most challenging problem in the world today? How would you address this problem? Write a 500-word essay about your approach.

This is WriteGirl!

www.writegirl.org

myself

This is WriteGirl

Founded in 2001, WriteGirl is a creative writing and mentoring organization that promotes creativity, critical thinking and leadership skills to empower teen girls. WriteGirl currently serves over 300 at-risk teen girls in Los Angeles County.

Its Core Mentoring Program is comprised of girls from 107 schools. WriteGirl pairs teen girls with professional women writers for one-on-one mentoring, workshops, public readings and publication in award-winning, nationally-distributed anthologies. WriteGirl also provides individual college, scholarship and financial aid guidance to every participant. For the tenth year in a row, 100% of teens participating in the WriteGirl Core Program have graduated from high school and enrolled in college.

The Power of 10! *WriteGirl celebrates 10 years.*

"Every year I'm in WriteGirl, I fall more
and more in love with words."
— A WriteGirl Mentee

WriteGirl teens are encouraged to speak their mind on the 'soapbox', a popular part of every workshop.

www.writegirl.org

WriteGirl mentors are accomplished novelists, journalists, poets, screenwriters, marketing professionals and more.

This anthology is the tenth publication from WriteGirl's Core Mentoring Program.

WriteGirl also brings weekly creative writing workshops to critically at-risk teen girls at schools in Arleta, Azusa, Compton, Lawndale, and South Los Angeles in its innovative In-Schools Program. In the past three years, the In-Schools Program has expanded to serve 150 girls at five Los Angeles County Office of Education (LACOE) Alternative Education Community Day Schools. Students at these schools are pregnant or parenting teens, foster youth, on probation, have social workers or are unable to return to their home schools due to any number of issues.

Through participation in WriteGirl, girls develop vital communication skills, self confidence, critical thinking skills, deeper academic engagement and enhanced creativity for a lifetime of increased opportunities.

Workshops

One Saturday each month, WriteGirl teens and women writers gather for a full day of writing. Workshops are led by professional women poets, screenwriters, songwriters, novelists and journalists. They are some of the most respected writers in their fields.

TV writers Diane Ruggerio and Nina Weinman-Swift give feedback to a girl at the Screenwriting Workshop.

At the Songwriting Workshop, guest singer/songwriters guide girls to write memorable lyrics, then set the girls' lyrics to music at the end of the day.

www.writegirl.org

Monthly workshops help women and girls to get to know each other as writers and friends.

Workshops are interactive and surprising. "Inspiration Stations" incorporate props that stimulate all five senses.

Many of the pieces found in this book started out as WriteGirl workshop experiments.

Special Guest Presenters and Mentors

Screenwriting Workshop

Writers:
Moira McMahon
Jan O'Connor
Gina Prince-Bythewood
Diane Ruggiero
Clare Sera
Nina Weinman-Swift

Actors:
Carly Craig
John Halbach
Porter Kelly
Amy Landecker
Retta Putignano
Mike Rock
Ryan Smith
Ellyn Stern
Ashley Summer

Los Angeles Times feature writer Deborah Vankin points out the differences between journalism and creative nonfiction.

Songwriting Workshop

Kyler England
Courtney Fortune
Laurie Geltman
Adrianne Gonzales
Keldamuzik
Michelle Lewis
Clare Means
Eve Nelson
Lindy Robbins
Lindsay Rush
Renee Stahl

Actors volunteer their time and talent to brings the girls' words to life onstage.

"Thanks to WriteGirl, I'm now motivated by strong, creative women, not just by deadlines!"

— A WriteGirl Mentor

Poetry Workshop

Xotchil-Julisa Bermejo
Gail Wronsky
Eloise Klein Healy

Performance Workshop

B.J. Dodge
Regina Louise

Fiction Workshop

Katie Alender
Robin Benway
Cecil Castellucci
Keren Essex
Jennifer Hunt
Margaret Stohl

Literary Panel (at Mentor Retreat)

Loraine Despres
Nicole Gregory
Margaret Stohl
Wendy West

Screenwriter Gina Prince-Bythewood at the annual Screenwriting Workshop.

Journalism/Creative Nonfiction Workshop

Tabby Biddle
Elaine Dutka
Dana Goodyear
Dora Herrera
Lina Lecaro
Maggie Nelson
Molly Palmer
Wendy Riche
Linda Toliver
Deborah Vankin

Lunch is a convivial part of every workshop and is donated by generous L.A. area restaurants and corporate donors.

Mentors guide girls through the college application process. For ten years in row, 1005 of participating WriteGirl seniors have gone on to college.

WriteGirl mentors all say that while they help girls to write, their own writing is re-invigorated in the process. It's a mutual learning process.

"Girls with purple hair. Girls with shaky voices. Girls with bold words. Girls stretching the limits of their minds and hearts. Girls with courage. Girls with dreams. Hip girls. Shy girls. Clever girls. Sweet, beautiful, budding bursts of talent and light—I love them all. Bravo WriteGirl!"

— A WriteGirl Mentor

Mentoring

WriteGirl matches professional women writers with teen girls for one-on-one mentoring in creative writing. Every week, mentoring pairs write at a coffee shops or libraries. They laugh, explore, create, reflect and inspire each other. WriteGirl screens, selects and trains writer-volunteers to empower girls by helping them find their unique voices. Mentor advisors provide support and help throughout the year. 150 women writers contribute 2,000 volunteer hours each month as mentors, workshop leaders and volunteers.

WriteGirl pairs in the Core Mentoring Program work together for an average of three years. Many stay in touch through college years and beyond.

"I didn't know she could write. In my culture, it's the men who write. My son wants to be a writer. So it's an unexpected and pleasant surprise about my daughter. It's the depth of her writing that surprises me for being 15. This experience has blossomed her to the degree that she's confident, and this program has enabled her to see there are no limits to what she can do."

— A WriteGirl Parent

Each nine-month WriteGirl season culminates in a high-energy celebration at the Writers Guild of America Theater in Beverly Hills. The event features a silent auction, lunch reception, special celebrity guests and a sneak preview of the next WriteGirl anthology.

WriteGirl teens performed at The Women's Conference at the Long Beach Convention Center before an audience of 14,000 attendees.

Performing at large events like the Los Angeles Times Festival of Books gives a girl increased confidence and self-esteem.

"This new light of confidence shines through when someone believes in me. I love receiving help from someone who actually cares. I trust WriteGirl, even more than my counselor."

Public Readings

WriteGirl teens read their work boldly at bookstores and book festivals all over the city. Their voices entertain and inspire audiences of friends, family and newcomers to WriteGirl.

Girls read their work in public to hone their performance skills.

"WriteGirl is helping her with her emotions. Alejandra is kind of quiet and now she can put her emotions into words. She finds some really beautiful words. They found my daughter's passion."

— A WriteGirl Parent

Publications

Since 2001, WriteGirl Publications has been producing award-winning anthologies that showcase the bold voices and imaginative insights of women and girls. Unique in both design and content, WriteGirl anthologies present a wide range of personal stories, poetry, essays, scenes and lyrics, as well as a selection of WriteGirl writing experiments to inspire readers to find their own creative voices.

Ten anthologies from WriteGirl showcase the work of over 1,000 women and girls. Selections range from serious to whimsical, personal to political, and heart-rending to uplifting.

WriteGirl anthologies have collectively won 30 national and international book awards. You should see the medals and certificates adorning our office!

Order WriteGirl books online from www.writegirl.org, from www.Amazon.com, or buy them in person from local bookstores nationwide.

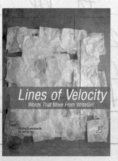

"My mentee continues to be lovely and illuminating. At this point I'm not actually sure who is mentoring whom!"
— A WriteGirl Mentor

write girl
www.writegirl.org

ForeWord Reviews, School Library Journal, Kirkus, Los Angeles Times Book Review, The Writer Magazine and *VOYA* have all raved about WriteGirl books.

"WriteGirl's wonderful, inspirational anthology [*Listen to Me*] belongs in every media center, public library and creative writing class."
　　— *VOYA* Magazine review

"Until girls from around the country can access the beauty in one-on-one mentoring and a varied writing education, each anthology from WriteGirl offers a small taste of the experience."
　　— *ForeWord* Magazine review

Pens on Fire, *WriteGirl's educator's guide, offers over 200 inspiring writing experiments for teens and adults. Through the innovative use of props, movement, art, music, textures, scents and even flavors,* **Pens on Fire** *offers step-by-step creative writing curricula for teachers and youth leaders.*

Bold Ink Awards

The WriteGirl Bold Ink Awards were created five years ago to honor the women who inspire our girls, our mentors and audiences around the world. We seek out storytellers whose voices move us. Their genres represent the breadth of our own membership and their achievements mark the degree of excellence we all strive for. They write in Bold Ink.

2011 Honorees:

Screenwriter/actor Nia Vardalos; TV writer/actor Sarah Silverman; screenwriter Winnie Holzman; TV writer Savannah Dooley; screenwriter Aline Brosh McKenna; songwriter Kara DioGuardi and WriteGirl Executive Director, Keren Taylor.

Honoree Aline Brosh McKenna (Devil Wears Prada, 27 Dresses) accepts her Bold Ink Award.

Flowers donated by Teleflora; drinks from POM, Barefoot Wine & Bubbly and Tru Vodka.

Past Bold Ink Award Honorees:

Wanda Coleman, Jennifer Crittenden, Diablo Cody, Liz Craft,
Sarah Fain, Janet Fitch, Carol Flint, Naomi Foner, Gigi Levangie,
Callie Khouri, Suzanne Lummis, Nancy Meyers, Patt Morrison,
Carol Muske-Dukes, Sonia Nazario, Gina Prince-Bythewood,
Lynda Resnick, Elizabeth Sarnoff, Carolyn See, Patricia Seyburn,
Marisa Silver, Mona Simpson, Jill Soloway, Robin Swicord,
Sandra Tsing Loh and Diane Warren.

Youth Leadership

WriteGirl develops leaders. Many WriteGirl alumnae serve as WriteGirl interns, gaining valuable planning, writing, management and marketing experience.

WriteGirl teens have won creative writing awards from Mayor Antonio Villaraigosa, the City of Los Angeles Department of Cultural Affairs and The Sally Picow Foundation.

"WriteGirl is the reason why I am able to communicate effectively. WriteGirl is the reason why I went to college. Every amazing, life-changing experience I've had so far is somehow tied back to WriteGirl because it catalyzed my personal growth..."

WriteGirl teens have been awarded scholarships from numerous colleges and the renowned Posse Foundation. This year, a WriteGirl teen became a Fulbright Scholar. WriteGirl teens were also featured panelists at the Geena Davis Institute for Gender in Media Conference and invited by the Women's Foundation of California to present a Momentum Award to Isabel Allende.

www.writegirl.org

Never underestimate the power of a girl and her pen!

"My love for WriteGirl is truly ineffable. WriteGirl's work goes beyond what you see on paper; it encourages young girls to expand their imagination as writers and as individuals."
— A WriteGirl Alumna

LEADERSHIP: THE WRITEGIRL "ENGINE"

Executive Director
Keren Taylor

Associate Director
Allison Deegan

Events and Operations
Reparata Mazzola

Membership Coordinator
Ali Prosch

In-Schools Program Coordinators
Katherine Thompson
Amber Caron

Workshops Coordinator
Kirsten Giles

Administrative Assistant
Kiran Puri

Public Relations
Rachel Wimberly

Event Assistants
Claire Baker
Naomi Buckley
Audrey Cain
Carey Campbell
Jodi Clark
Allison Longton
Lindsay Mendoza
Ashley Reid
Staci Roberts

Silent Auctions
Retta Putignano

WriteGirl Alumnae Interns
Leonor Cedano
Ariel Edwards-Levy
Shayne Holtzman
Rachel Hogue
Ashley Simone Lee

High School Interns
Jackelyne Cuellar
Jenny Gonzalez

Special thanks to the Constitutional Rights Foundation for the placement and supervision of committed teens interning with WriteGirl.

Website, Branding, Book Design, Graphics
Sara Apelkvist, Erin Fleiner, Nathalie Gallmeier, Yass Nassiri, Juliana Sankaran-Felix

Photography/Videography
Lisa Beebe, Jami Biven, BLT Helps, Clayton Goodfellow, Thomas Hargis, Laura Hoopes, Margaret Hyde, Mario de Lopez, Ryan Philips, Tiffany Peterson, Luther Scott, Rachel Werth, Shazia Wilson, Marvin Yan

WriteGirl Volunteers

Maia Akiva
Abby Anderson
Amy Aniobi
Diane Avila
Erika Ayon
Annie Azzariti
Porschia Baker
Sarine Balian
Lesley Balla
Justine Barron
Carol Bathke
Lisa Beebe
Alyson Beecher
Bonnie Berry LaMon
Christine Bevins
Natasha Billawala
Lara Boyko
Anita Brenner
Belle Bromfield
Annie Brown
Julie Buchwald
Sarah Burghauser
Emily Carroll
Rebecca Cathcart
Kathleen Cecchin
Cindy Collins
Catherine Cook
Jia-Rui Cook
Jeanine Cornillot
Becky Dale
Irene Daniel
Jessica Dean
Tracy DeBrincat
Anna Denee
Beverly Dennis
Loraine Despres
Jamie Diamond
Kathleen DiPerna
Julia Drake
Tina Dupuy
Elaine Dutka
Amanda Elend
Faith England
Simona Erlikh
Rachel Fain

Annette Farmer
Kimberly Fero
Susanne Ferrull
Toni Fields
Linda Folsom
Khanisha Foster
Judy Fox
Mimi Freedman
Melisa Garcia
Kate Garsson
Trina Gaynon
Kim Genkinger
Deborah George
Latrisse Goffigan
Estella Gonzalez
Jessy Goodman
Jane Gov
Arlene Granadosin
Jazmine Green
Jennifer Hanson
Erika Hayasaki
Molly Hennessy-Fiske
Deirdre Higgins
Laura Hightower
Alison Hills
Mona Holmes-Nisker
Jennifer Hummer
Margaret Hyde
Ashaki Jackson
Brande Jackson
Janet Jackson
Katie Jacobson
Becca Jensen
Jennifer Johnson
Lauren Johnson
Anissa Johnson
Cindy Jones
Jen Jones
Porter Kelly
Cowy Kim
Megan Kimble
Jody Rosen Knower
Cynthia Knox
Kendra Kozen
Tanja Laden

Raechal Leone
Jacqueline Lesko
Pamela Levy
Emily Lewis
Michelle Lewis
Elline Lipkin
Andrea Lwin
Michele Maher
Lauren Marks
Sarah McBride
Margo McCall
Adesuwa McCalla
Caitlin McIntyre
Jessica McKay
Claudia Melatini
Candice Merkson
Brittany Michelson
Carly Milne
Orly Minazad
Maureen Moore
Nicole Morris
Shanon Muir
Christine Murphy Bevins
Sandra O'Briant
Jennifer Oldham
Jazmin Ortega
Kimberly Page
Stephanie Parent
Jackie Parker
Katy Parks-Wilson
Nandita Patel
Janae Patino
Amanda Pendolino
Katie Peterson
Hunter Phillips
Elda Pineda
Natalie Poston
Darby Price
Retta Putignano
Marni Rader
India Radfar
Anthea Raymond
Ashley Reid
Laura Rhinehart
Glenda Richardson

Emily Richmond
Jane Robbins
Berna Roberts
Staci Roberts
Teresa Rochester
Jennifer Rowland
Marytza Rubio
Alicia Ruskin
Pamela Russell
Jennifer Rustigian
Melissa Ryan
Joanne Sala
Jasmine Salters
Vera Santamaria
Katherine Satorius
Gisel Saumat
Beth Schacter
Nicole Sconiers
Alicia Sedwick
Clare Sera
Gayle Shulman
Inez Singletary
Hemmy So
Lynn Soban
Laura Spain
Chelsea Steiner
Kit Steinkellner
Barbara Stimson
Samantha Stratton
Dana Stringer
Bonita Thompson
Rachel Torres
Selma Turgut
Dana Valenzuela
Valencia Walker
Adrienne Walser
Kristen Waltman
Zahirah Washington
Krysta Whittemore
Jacqueline Wilson
Melissa Wong
Sandy Yang
Amber Yee
Christina Ying

AWARDS/ COMMENDATIONS FOR KEREN TAYLOR AND WRITEGIRL

2011	President's National Youth, Arts and Humanities Program Awards, Finalist
2011	Women Making a Difference Award, Los Angeles Business Journal, Finalist
2010- 2011	California Nonprofit of the Year Award and Medal for Service
2010	Humanitas Philanthropy Prize
2010	Azusa Unified School District Certificate of Appreciation
2010	Annenberg Alchemy Leadership Champion
2010	Ruby Award, Women Helping Women, Soroptimist International
2009	California Governor and First Lady's Nonprofit Leader Medal for Service, Finalist
2009	Springfield College School of Human Services Community Hero Award
2008	President's Volunteer Call to Service Award
2008	Community Woman of Achievement, Business & Professional Women Hollywood
2008	Women Making a Difference Award, Los Angeles Business Journal, Finalist
2008	Certificate of Appreciation, Los Angeles Mayor Antonio Villaraigosa
2008	Coming Up Taller Award, President's Arts and Humanities Committee, Semi-Finalist
2007	Certificate of Appreciation, Los Angeles Mayor Antonio Villaraigosa
2006	Soroptimist International, Making a Difference for Women Award
2006	Certificate of Achievement, Los Angeles Mayor Antonio Villaraigosa
2006	Governor Arnold Schwarzenegger Commendation Letter
2006	Senator Gilbert Cedillo, 2nd District of CA, Commendation
2006	Gloria Molina, Supervisor, 1st District of California, Commendation
2006	Fabian Nunez, Speaker of the Assembly, Certification of Recognition
2006	Congressman Ed Reyes, 1st District of Los Angeles, Commendation
2005	Certificate of Appreciation, Los Angeles Mayor Antonio Villaraigosa
2004	President's Volunteer Call to Service Award

COMMUNITY CONNECTIONS

Participating Schools:

Agoura High School

Alverno High School

Anahuacalmeca High School

Animo Venice Charter High School

Azusa High School

Bell High School

Birmingham Community
Charter High School

Bishop Montgomery High School

Burbank High School

Cabrillo High School

Calabasas High School

CALS Early College High School

Central Los Angeles High School #9

Cerritos High School

Chaminade College Preparatory
Academy

CHAMPS

City Honors High School

Claremont High School

Covina High School

Crossroads School

Culver City High School

Dana Middle School

Daniel Pearl Magnet High School

Dexter High School

Dorsey High School

Eagle Rock High School

Foothill Country Day School

Foshay Learning Center

Frank D. Parent High School

Frederick Douglass Academy

Freemont High School

Garden Grove High School

Garfield High School

George Washington
Preparatory High School

Gertz Ressler High School

Grant High School

Hamilton High Academy of Music

Hamilton High School

Harvard Westlake School

Hawthorne Middle School

Highland Hall

Hollywood High School

Holy Family Grade School

Huntington Park High School

Immaculate Conception

Immaculate Heart High School

Incarnation School

International Studies Learning Center

John Burroughs High School

John Marshall Fundamental High
School

John Marshall High School

King Drew Magnet
High School of Medicine

L.A. Center for Enriched Studies
(LACES)

L.A. County High School for the Arts

La Mirada High School

Lincoln Middle School

Linden Center

Los Angeles Leadership Academy

Los Osos High School

Lynwood High School

Manual Arts High School
Mark Keppel High School
Marlborough School
Miguel Contreras Learning
Complex School
Mira Costa High School
New Millennium High School
New Roads High School
New Village Charter High School
Notre Dame Academy
Opportunities for Learning
Options for Youth
Orange County High School of the
Arts
Oscar de la Hoya Animo
Charter High School
Palisades Charter High School
Pasadena High School
Polytechnic High School
Port of Los Angeles High School
Porter Middle School
Providence High School
Ralston Intermediate School
Ramona Convent School
Renaissance High School for the Arts
Richard Gahr High School
Richardson Middle School
San Marino High School
Sherman Oaks Center
for Enriched Studies
Sierra Canyon School
South Hills High School
St. Mary's Academy

Sunland Christian School
Sussman Middle School
Temple City High School
The Rosemary School
University High School
Verdugo Hills High School
View Park Preparatory
Charter High School
Vista Mar School
Walter Reed Middle School
West Adams Preparatory
High School
West High School
Westchester High School
Whittier High School

Referring Organizations:

Antioch University Los Angeles
Constitutional Rights Foundation

Fox Gives

Idealist.org

Los Angeles Times Festival of Books

PEN Center USA West

UCLA Extension Writers' Program

United Way of Ventura

VolunteerMatch

West Hollywood Book Fair

The Women's Conference

Writers Guild of America, West

Writers Guild of America Foundation

WRITEGIRL SUPPORTERS

WriteGirl would like to thank all of our **individual donors** who have so generously contributed to help us grow and help more teen girls each year.

We would also like to thank the following **foundations, government entities** and **corporations** for their support:

19 Entertainment
ABC Family
Adams Family Foundation
Ahmanson Foundation
American Association of University Women
Amazon.com
Annenberg Foundation
Bad Robot Productions
Band From TV
Bloomspot
BLT & Associates
Boone Family Foundation
Borders
Capital Group
Citrin Cooperman
City of Los Angeles Cultural Affairs Department, Youth Arts and Education Program
Creative Artists Agency
DIRECTV
Disney
Dwight Stuart Youth Foundation
Edlow Family Fund
Eisner Foundation
FACE Stockholm
Fox
Frog Crossing Foundation
5 For Fairness
Gilman Family Trust
Goodworks Foundation
Granta
The Green Foundation
Guitar Center
Hay Foundation
The Humanitas Prize
J.R. Hyde III Family Foundation

ICM
iGive
Kikkerland
The Los Angeles Sparks
Literary Lab
Los Angeles County Office of Education
Los Angeles Unified School District – Beyond the Bell Branch
Mozaic Media
NBC Universal Foundation
Oder Family Foundation
Pacific Life Foundation
Paradigm
Ralph M. Parsons Foundation
Playtone
Simon and Diana Raab Foundation
Ralphs
Rare Bird Lit
RDWM USA
Roll International
RR Donnelley
San Gennaro Foundation
Sony
Soroptimist International
Southern California Edison
Marc and Eva Stern Foundation
Thruline Entertainment
Time Warner
United Talent Agency
Weingart Foundation
Wiles Magazine
WME
Women's Foundation of California
Women Helping Youth
Writers Guild of America, West
Ziffren Brittenham LLC

OUR SPECIAL THANKS TO

All of WriteGirl's mentors and volunteers for professional services, including strategic planning, public relations, event coordination, mentoring management, training & curriculum development, catering, financial management and administrative assistance.

Advisory Board Members for their support and guidance on strategy, fundraising, communications and development of community partnerships.

The Honorable Mayor Antonio Villaraigosa; Los Angeles Council members Eric Garcetti, Tom LaBonge and **Jan Perry**; and **First Lady Maria Shriver** for their support and acknowledgement of WriteGirl's contributions to the community.

Los Angeles Unified School District, Beyond the Bell Division and **the Miguel Contreras Learning Center** for providing a workshop space where over 150 women and girls gather to write each month. Yucca Community Center, GRAMMY Foundation, Volunteer Assistance League of Southern California and the Writers Guild of America for event space.

Book Expo America, Los Angeles Times Festival of Books, Skylight Books, West Hollywood Book Fair, and **UCLA Writers Faire** for donating WriteGirl space and promotional support at these events.

Writing Journals: Harry Abrams, Blick Art Materials, BrushDance Inc., Carolina Pads, Cavallini Papers & Co., Chronicle Books, Ecojot, Falling Water, Fiorentina, Flavia, Galison/MudPuppy Press, Hartley and Marks, JournalBooks, Kikkerland Design, Anne McGilvray & Company, Michael Roger Press, Mirage Paper Company, Retired Hipster, Rock Scissor Paper, Running Rhino & Co., K. Schweitzer, Trends International, Whimsy Press.

Food, Dessert and Beverages at WriteGirl Workshops and Special Events: Bagel Broker, Barefoot Wine & Bubbly, Barragan's Mexican Restaurant, Big Sugar Bakeshop, Border Grill, Carol Martin Cupcakes, Chef Gordon Smith, Chipotle, Cookie Casa, Cuties, Earth Wind and Flour, El Pollo Loco, Frankie's on Melrose, IZZE Beverages, Kychon Chicken, La Pizza Loca, Les Macarons Duverger, Little Caesar's Pizza, Louise's Trattoria, Mani's Bakery, Kate Mantilini, Maria's Italian Kitchen, Masa of Echo Park, Michael's Restaurant, Mozza, Musso and Franks, Nestle Juicy Juice, Olive Garden, Panda Restaurant Group, Panera Bread, Pescado Mojado, Platine Cookies, POM Wonderful, Porto's Bakery,

Ralphs, Real Food Daily, Señor Fish, Sharky's Woodfire Grill, Spitz, SusieCakes, The Riverside Café, TRU Vodka, Tudor House, Veggie Grill, Yuca's and all of our volunteers who donated delicious desserts for our workshops.

Gifts for Members and Event Donors: 55 Degree Wine, ABC Family, Abra Therapeutics, Bauble Bath, Beacon Hotel, Blackwell Fitness, Blue Planet Soap Company, Daisy Rock Guitar, Design Printing, DIRECTV, Disney, Dr. Bronner's Magic Soaps, Earthly Body, Earthpack, EK Success, EOS, Evan Healy Cosmetics, Everybody's Nuts, FACE Stockholm, Flemming Chalef, Flex Flop, Fox Regency Pictures, Fox Searchlight, Fox Home Entertainment, Four Seasons Hotel, Glee Gum/Verve, Good Cheer Company, Hilton Checkers Hotel, Hint Mints, Home Collective, ICU eyewear, Intercontinental Hotel, Jakks Pacific, JousJous.com, Kiss Me in the Garden, Kitsch*n Glam, Kikkerland, Kirana Skin Care Clinic, Klean Bath & Body, Cindy Lauren, Little Mismatched, Linco Picture Framing, Magnetic Poetry, Mo's Nose, Murad Skin Care Products, Nancy's Creation, NBC Universal, Nektar De Stagni, Neutrogena, Noodle Talk, Organic Essence, Oriental Trading Co., PakNak, Parlux Fragrances, Pentel, Pharmaca, Quotable Cards, Re-Mi Vintage, Roll, Sacred Heart LA, Santa Monica Writers' Junction, Soolip Paperie Press, Southern California Beauty Supplies, The Story Society, Tarte, Teleflora, Tema, Two's Company, Vietri, Writers Boot Camp, Zest Books.

Printing and Copy Services: Chromatic Lithographers Inc., FedEx Office, RR Donnelley, Burdge Cooper, UPrinting.

Website/Branding: **Fabric Interactive** and **Sara Apelkvist** for design and branding strategy, including development of WriteGirl's logo, website, press kit, stationery, publications and ongoing support.

Maia Akiva is a magical realism writer, originally from Israel. Her plays *life* and *I hate love* are published by Brooklyn Publishers. Her short stories are published in *Bewildering Stories*, *Diverse Voices Quarterly* and *Spirits Literary Magazine*. You can find her and her writing at: www.selfhelpfiction.net

Erika Ayón emigrated from Mexico when she was five years old. She grew up in South Central Los Angeles and graduated from UCLA with a B.A. in English. She was selected as a 2009 PEN-Rosenthal Emerging Voices Fellow. Erika has taught poetry workshops thoughout Los Angeles.

Claire Baker is an artist and teacher, and Program Assistant in the WriteGirl In-Schools Program. She received her M.F.A. in Painting and Drawing at UCLA. Claire currently teaches painting as adjunct faculty at California State University, Long Beach. She received a Pollock-Krasner Foundation Grant for 2011 to pursue her drawing.

Porschia Librecht Baker envisions utilizing words' agency to create breakthroughs in herself and crevices in whoever is witnessing. Currently, she's an M.F.A. student in the Interdisciplinary Arts program at Goddard College.

Sarine Balian writes creative non-fiction, poetry and fiction. "An Airplane Over Our Home, My Mother..." from her from her collection of memoir/ creative non-fiction about growing up in Lebanon was published in *The Village Rambler* (May/June 2005), and she received the Stanford University Writer's Studio Continuing Studies Fellowship.

Carol Bathke, a recently retired educator, worked with English Learner students from many countries at a large high school in the L.A. area. She also has experience in writing university research reports and grant applications.

When **Lisa Beebe** isn't volunteering with WriteGirl, she blogs and writes personality quizzes for TeenNick.com. She is currently working on her first novel.

Natasha Billawala believes everyone has a tale to tell. Working in television always been her passion, and she enjoys not only the writing of it, but also studying its history. Writing on the show *Everwood* remains her favorite experience. She is currently helping to write a pilot for AMC and developing many projects for both film and TV.

Lara Boyko is a freelance sportswriter whose work has appeared on Sports Illustrated.com, NCAA.com and AVP.com.

Annie Brown, an East Coast transplant, teaches history and English at S.T.E.M. Academy in Los Angeles. She has a Master's degree in education from Harvard and recently started an educational consulting business. She enjoys writing poetry and narrative non-fiction.

Julie Buchwald holds a B.A. from Northwestern University in philosophy and international studies, and a J.D. from the University of Southern California. By day, she writes reviews of shooting investigations for the Los Angeles Police Commission's Office of the Inspector General. By night, she writes her novel – a cross between *C.S.I.*, *Spin City*, and *Sex and the City*.

Amber Caron is the WriteGirl In-Schools Workshop Leader at Arleta and Azusa Community Day Schools. Prior to her work with WriteGirl, she taught in the Virginia public schools, at Northeastern University, and at the Governor's School of North Carolina. She holds an M.A. from Northeastern University and a B.A. from the University of Hartford.

Emily Carroll fell in love with figurative language in the 6th grade when one of her classmates wrote, "war is like a dull pencil; there's no point." Ever since, she has been captivated by the magic and beauty of language.

Cindy Collins has a B.A. in Journalism from the University of Arizona and writes short stories, scripts and Web content. This is her fifth year as a WriteGirl volunteer.

Jia-Rui Chong Cook is a science writer at NASA's Jet Propulsion Laboratory. She writes about ice volcanoes on Saturn's moon Titan, the strange behavior of the solar wind at the edge of the solar system and giant asteroids. She keeps a blog about travels near and far at http://postmarkhere.wordpress.com.

Tracy DeBrincat's award-winning short stories and poetry have been published in literary journals from *Another Chicago Magazine* to *Zyzzyva*. Her fiction collection, *Moon Is Cotton & She Laugh All Night*, was published in 2010 by Subito Press.

Anna Denee is a published songwriter and emerging poet. She is currently performing at local shows and working on a book of poetry.

Beverly Dennis is a successful educational consultant who writes, designs, and develops online and hybrid learning experiences for K-12 students. She is also a professor and is working on a book for parents of children with learning disabilities.

Kathleen DiPerna is a television writer/producer and member of the Writers Guild of America. She has worked as a lyricist in both songwriting and commercial jingles. Kathleen is a regular contributor to spoken word events and online media publications and is currently working on her first screenplay.

Rachel Fain's second grade teacher predicted she'd be a high school dropout, because she wrote pages and pages every week, and, as a result, didn't finish her "alphabet stories." Her teacher was wrong. Today Rachel is a writer and editor, and much better at meeting deadlines.

This is **Kimberly Fero**'s first year volunteering with WriteGirl. She has a B.A. in English and Dance from CSU Fullerton and a Graduate Certificate in Publishing from University of Denver. She works as a technical writer/editor in Orange County.

Toni Fields is an actress and writer from Detroit, Michigan. She now resides in Orange County. She studied at the American Academy of Dramatic Arts and the Detroit Repertory Theatre. She is currently writing songs for and collaborating with a popular R&B artist.

Linda Folsom, a graduate of UCLA, has been an Imagineer for eighteen years, leader of the WDI writers group for seven and WriteGirl mentor for the past four. She embraces the Internet, using it for writing prompts and as a platform for her Empty Nest blog.

Judy Fox is a freelance writer who specializes in writing grants for universities and educated-related nonprofits. In her free time, she writes short stories and reads voraciously.

Melisa Garcia is a poet in her fourth year at the University of California, Riverside majoring in creative writing and Spanish literature with a minor in women's studies. After graduating, she hopes to go to grad school and translate Central American poetry.

Trina Gaynon, in addition to volunteering for WriteGirl, volunteers for an Orange County literacy program. She has Master's degrees from UC Berkeley (library sciences) and USF (creative writing). Her poems recently appeared in the literary journals *Cloudbank* and *Thirty First Bird Review*, as well as the anthology *Knocking at the Door*.

Kim Genkinger is a Creative Director/Writer for Roll Global's in-house advertising agency, Fire Station. Her clients include POM Wonderful, Wonderful Pistachios, California Cuties, Teleflora and FIJI Water, to name a few. There's a good chance you've TIVO'd through her work.

Before coming to Los Angeles, **Kirsten Giles** lived in Kentucky, Mexico City, Honolulu, and on a small farm in northern California. When she's not creating poetry, she develops training programs and learning games for a variety of corporate clients.

Estella Gonzalez is a writer from East L.A. whose fiction and poetry have been published in various literary magazines and anthologies including *Puerto del Sol*, *1111* and *Latinos in Lotusland: An Anthology of Contemporary Southern California Literature*. She has a story forthcoming in *Huizache Literary Magazine*.

Jessy Goodman works as a writer/editor at a national magazine, and will begin graduate school to earn her M.F.A. in fiction this fall. She is currently revising her first novel, *A State of Arrested Decay*, and loves to travel in search of inspiring settings for her creative work.

Jane Gov earned a B.A. in creative writing and a Master's of library and information science. She is a fiction writer, librarian, former bookstore manager, and a book group leader. She is currently working on a YA fantasy novel.

Arlene Granadosin is a reborn writer living in Pasadena who recently rediscovered a focus on writing as a ritual. She has a background in urban planning and history, which, in more ways than one, influences her poetry, short stories, and non-fiction articles.

Erika Hayasaki spent nearly a decade as a reporter covering news and writing feature stories for the *Los Angeles Times*, where she was a staff metro reporter, education writer, and New York-based national correspondent. She is currently writing her first book while teaching at the University of California, Irvine.

Molly Hennessy-Fiske is a metro staff writer for the *Los Angeles Times*. She headed to Afghanistan this year after reporting tours in Baghdad, D.C., a Reuters fellowship in Beirut and a Pew fellowship in Mexico. Molly graduated from Harvard College in 1999.

Laura Hightower has worked as an editor and freelance writer, as well as in marketing, public relations, and communications. Currently, she is a graduate student at the University of Southern California, where she is pursuing advanced degrees in education and English.

Rachel Hogue is an alumna of the WriteGirl Core Mentoring Program, and has recently begun to volunteer for the organization that greatly enriched her life as a young woman. Her writing can be seen in several WriteGirl anthologies. Rachel will be continuing her education at CSU Sacramento this fall.

Ashaki Jackson is a social psychologist, editor, and poet. *Torch Journal*, *The Drunken Boat*, *Cave Canem*, and *Suisun Valley Review* – among other publications – have featured her work.

Brande Jackson runs *Living Histories*, a small arts-based nonprofit that provides afterschool programming, and *Lokahi*, an organization that provides campaign management services. She also teaches community-based art and creativity classes, and is a part-time lecturer at Cal State University, Fullerton.

Janet Alston Jackson's memoir, *A Cry for Light: A Journey Into Love*, won the National USA Book News Award for Christian Inspiration. She is a personal growth expert and behavioral consultant for her company Sporting the Right Attitude.

Katie Jacobson is from New Jersey, and didn't know about the existence of unincorporated areas until age 20. Thus, she is fascinated by rurality and being in the middle of nowhere. She is currently working on a collection of stories about people with biological abnormalities. Her writing is featured in valeveil's CASEBOK/Ekphrasis project.

Anissa Johnson is a freelance writer and producer in reality television. She has worked with companies such as MTV Networks, Mark Burnett Productions and New Regency Productions. She was also the recipient of The Guy Hanks and Marvin Miller Screenwriting Fellowship.

Cindy Jones is a published writer with an M.F.A. in writing. Her work includes numerous short stories and short films. Her recent project *Love Letter* was produced as a USC graduate thesis film and her short story "Undertow" was published in the New York based quarterly *Alt Pick*.

Porter Kelly is an L.A.-based actor/writer. Acting credits include *The Office*, *Lie to Me*, *Private Practice* and many more. Porter wrote sketch comedy for Acme Saturday Night for three years. Look for her CGI alter ego in the highly anticipated video game "L.A. Noire". www.porterkelly.com

Jody Rosen Knower writes and edits all manner of nonfiction. Her work has appeared in *New Jersey Monthly*, *MAMM Magazine*, and *Publishers Weekly*. She is a graduate of Columbia University's Graduate School of Journalism and the author of a long-running blog.

Kendra Kozen is an award-winning journalist whose work appears in print and online. A native New Yorker, she received a master's degree from the University of Southern California in 2006 and has called Los Angeles home for almost a decade.

Emily Lewis is a Los Angeles-based writer. She has written for television (*The Shield*), magazines (*Whole Life Times*) and numerous online publications. Currently, she crafts messaging for an entertainment company when not outlining her first memoir, expanding her jewelry line or ridding the world of cat hair.

Elline Lipkin is a writer whose first book of poems, *The Errant Thread*, was published with Kore Press, and first nonfiction book, *Girls' Studies*, was published by Seal Press. She blogs for *Ms.* magazine and *Girl w/Pen: Bridging Feminist Research & Popular Culture*.

Allison Longton is an Event Assistant and In-Schools Program Assistant for WriteGirl. She graduated from Texas State University with a theatre degree and, when not working at WriteGirl, is actively pursuing an acting career, taking classes at The Groundlings, where she writes sketch comedy.

Brooklyn-born **Reparata Mazzola** is a published book author (*Mafia Kingpin*), a produced screenwriter and an Emmy-nominated television writer/producer. As a member of Barry Manilow's back-up trio, Lady Flash, she toured the world and can be heard on seven of his albums and seen on several TV specials. Currently, she has two films in development.

Sarah McBride is a Los Angeles-based journalist. Her work has appeared in *The Wall Street Journal* and on National Public Radio.

Jessica McKay is a fifth grade Language Arts teacher at Center for Early Education. She holds a B.A. from Spelman College in English and an M.A. from Columbia University Teachers College in English education. She loves writing poetry and creative non-fiction.

Megan Kimble is a nonfiction writer and editor whose news and feature articles have appeared in the *Los Angeles Times*. She graduated from the University of Denver, and is currently editing a compilation book of stories from Skid Row in downtown Los Angeles.

Lauren Marks is a NYU graduate, and spent a decade working in professional theatre, pursuing her Ph.D. at CUNY. In 2007, she suffered a brain aneurysm, which radically altered her abilities to speak, read, and write. Her book-in-progress is a memoir entitled *A Stitch of Time: Portrait of a Mind in Construction*.

Claudia Melatini is a novelist and playwright. Her play *English Lessons*, received a staged reading at the award-winning Production Company Theatre. Her one-act *Scrub My Tub*, was a finalist in the Summer Sizzle One-Act Play Festival and was recently published by Original Works Publishing.

Candice Merkson has worked in the information technology field for the past eleven years with an emphasis in healthcare. She is currently working on publishing a poetry book titled *Letters from the Soul*. Writing poetry has been a way for her to express her true self, and share her love of poetry with others.

Maureen Moore is a travel writer, blogger, and translator. Having contributed to travel websites while living abroad, she now spends her time on personal writing projects inspired by the authors she works with at the Library Foundation's ALOUD series.

Hunter Phillips is Principal/CEO of Free Radical Pictures and just directed her comedic pilot, *Gym Ratz*. Phillips also works as a writer/producer for Stargreetz, a viral/mobile entertainment and marketing company. Other than working with WriteGirl, Hunter's favorite gig was as Neil Simon's writing assistant at the Geffen Playhouse.

Elda Pineda is a Los Angeles native who writes about Midwestern animals. She works in arts education and is proud to have been a WriteGirl volunteer for the past 3 years.

Katia Portillo-Valí started writing when she was 14 and studied at Pasadena City College and Los Angeles City College. She recently did research for Douglas Saunders for a non-fiction book, *Arrival City*, which will be published later in 2011.

Originally from Chicago, **Marietta (Retta) Putignano King** has been a WriteGirl mentor and Silent Auction Chair for six years. She writes and performs sketch comedy, and as co-owner of Create Your Reel, has written over 2,000 scenes for actors' reels.

Marni Rader crafts corporate marketing communication by day and devours Sherman Oaks Library books by night. When not in servitude to her dogs Tinker and Tula, she relishes delicious word craft with her brilliant mentee Zoe and the delightfully effervescent WriteGirl family at their illuminating workshops.

India Radfar is a poet with four published books of poetry on small presses, most recently *Position & Relation*, 2009, Station Hill Press. She teaches for California Poets in the Schools and is training to be a Certified Applied Poetry Therapy Facilitator for the National Association for Biblio/Poetry Therapy.

Sandra Ramos O'Briant's work has appeared in *LiteraryMama, Posse, Whistling Shade, Flashquake, Café Irreal*, and has been anthologized in *What Wildness is This: Women Write About the Southwest, Latinos in Lotus Land: An Anthology of Contemporary Southern California Literature, Hit List: The Best of Latino Mystery*, and *The Mom Egg*.

Glenda L. Richardson has worked as a professional writer since 2002. Her career began as an editor for a monthly publication in Durham, NC. Currently, Glenda works at BET Networks as part of an in-house writing team for scripted programming.

Berna Roberts' career spans nearly two decades. She is a regular on the SciFi Channel and the film festival circuit. She is also the owner of Foresight Management. She is currently working on a stage show that explores her inner nerd.

Jennifer Rowland began her professional life as a journalist covering politics and education. She currently works as a communication director for an independent school in Los Angeles.

When not working as a partner in a full service bi-coastal talent agency, **Alicia Ruskin** writes fiction, poetry and essays. She is a graduate of Brandeis University, The London Academy of Music and Dramatic Arts and the Sorbonne.

Pamela August Russell is the author of *B is for Bad Poetry*, out now from Sterling Publishing. The *Los Angeles Times* says "It may not be Walt Whitman, but Miss Russell's verses are often a whole lot funnier." Her short stories and poetry have appeared in several anthologies including *Virgin Territory* and most recently *Nothing Moments*. She lives in Los Angeles near the freeway.

Gisel Saumat moved from Miami, Florida to L.A. to pursue a career in film. She recently graduated with her Master's in psychology and is currently working on writing her first book and screenplay. She will be traveling to Thailand to teach English at the end of this year.

Beth Schacter is a film and TV writer living in Los Angeles.

Inez Singletary, shushed in her youth, started writing to hear her thoughts. Paper never protested her voice. She writes to see, examine and create her life. In 2008, her book, *Making What Your Means Can't Buy*, was published. It is a guide to making something from nothing. She loves WriteGirl.

Kit Steinkellner created the pilot *21st Century Horror Show* for Teen Nickelodeon and has written additional material for several Disney Channel Original Movies. Her work has been produced Off Broadway at Playwrights Horizons, the Kennedy Center, the San Diego Old Globe, and several theaters in Los Angeles.

Katherine Thompson is a poet, essayist, and teacher, originally from North Carolina. She holds a B.A. in English from Duke University and an M.A. in English Education from Wake Forest University. This is her second season as the In-Schools Program Coordinator for WriteGirl.

Rachel Torres is a product manager who has loved every bit of her 4 seasons with WriteGirl, especially writing with her sublime mentee, Jaclyn.

Selma Turgut is an R.N., and also has experience teaching high school English. She writes to fully understand herself and the world around her. Selma believes writing can capture the deepest part of ourselves and make us feel completely satiated.

Jacqueline Wilson, a proud New Yorker, began her television career at Nickelodeon as a Promo Writer/Producer. Currently, she works as a Supervising Story Producer on reality series such as *Basketball Wives* and *RuPaul's Drag Race*. She's a graduate of Syracuse University and recipient of the prestigious Bill Cosby screenwriting fellowship.

Rachel Wimberly has been writing since she could hold a pen, working with CNN Business News, *The New York Times* Regional Newspaper Group, *Variety Magazine* and she currently is editor-in-chief of the Trade Show News Network. Rachel is a 6-year member of WriteGirl and Director of Public Relations for the organization.

Melissa Wong is a television writer living in Los Angeles, specializing in live variety shows. Her credits include the MTV Movie Awards and the People's Choice Awards with host Queen Latifah. This is her fourth year as a mentor for WriteGirl.

Jennifer Wright is a Los Angeles-based writer and holds a B.S. in psychology from University of Illinois. She has been a contributor to *Tiny Buddha* and writes personal essays.

Christina Ying is an aspiring writer, theater artist, and youth advocate from San Francisco. She has a B.A. in Asian American Studies and looks forward to one day getting an M.F.A in creative writing.

A

Aguilar, Julie 30
Alfakey, Yasmine 206
Alonzo, Linda 171
Anderson, Calia 53
Anderson, Maya E. 77
Anderson, Christina Gabrielle 121
Antunez, Juliette 105
Ayuso, Jennifer 179

B

Ballesteros, Melanie 103
Barker, Kamryn 50
Barleta, Charice 25
Beebe, Lisa 216
Billawala, Natasha 89
Blackwell, Ciara 110
Bolton-Ford, Kathi 153
Brown, Annie 226
Burdorf, Rachel 232
Burnley, Zzzahkia 122
Burnley, Zzzzah-Zzaz 197
Burns, Jenna 146

C

Camp, Zoe Isabella 170
Carberry, Majah 234
Caron, Amber 228
Carrion, Vasti 60
Carroll, Emily 218
Castillo, Alejandra 70
Cerritos, Edna 152
Chambers, Kiarra 111
Cho, Alice 34

Cole, Jaclyn 205
Collins, Cindy 97
Cook, Jia-Rui 29
Cooper, Jatori 33
Crenshaw, Imani 235
Cuellar, Jackelyne 127
Curran, Tessa 157
Curtis, Jala' 183

D

Davis, Jillian 134
De Los Angeles, Gabriela 198
DeBrincat, Tracy 175
Deegan, Allison 135
Delva, Brittany 169
Dion, Hadley 176
DiPerna, Kathleen 123
Downs, Nichelle 73

e

Epperhart, Amy 140
Evans, Gabriella 104

F

Fain, Rachel 86
Fero, Kimberly 215
Fields, Toni 39
Fisher, Jamai 115
Flores, Danielle E. 138
Folkes, Lexy 191
Folsom, Linda 55
Francis, Jalisa 143

ABOUT THE PUBLISHER/EDITOR
AND WRITEGIRL LEADERSHIP

Keren Taylor, founder and Executive Director of WriteGirl, has been active as a community leader for more than 15 years. She has edited and designed dozens of anthologies and has served as publisher and editor of all of WriteGirl's award-winning books. Passionate about helping women and girls, Keren has conducted hundreds of creative writing workshops for youth and adults, and has led staff development workshops for the California Paraeducators Conference, California School-age Consortium, California Department of Education, Los Angeles County Office of Education, L.A.'s BEST and the New York Partnership for After School Education, among others. Keren has been selected to serve as a Community Champion and facilitator for the Annenberg Alchemy Program and is a popular speaker at conferences and book festivals nationwide, including the Association of Writing Programs (AWP) Annual Conference, BOOST Conference, *Los Angeles Times* Festival of Books and Guiding Lights Festival. Keren is the recipient of numerous awards and accolades, including the President's Volunteer Call to Service Award, Business & Professional Women's Community Woman of Achievement Award, Soroptomist International's Woman of Distinction Award, commendations from Los Angeles Mayor Antonio Villaraigosa and others.

Keren is an assemblage artist and mosaicist. Her artwork has been exhibited at the The Annex L.A., Barnsdall Art Center, Gallery 727, Rock Rose Gallery and Shambhala Center Los Angeles, and is in personal collections. Her assemblage works are featured on the book covers of WriteGirl anthologies. She holds a Bachelor's Degree in International Relations from the University of British Columbia, a Piano Performance Degree from the Royal Conservatory of Music, Toronto and a Diploma from the American Music and Dramatic Academy, New York City. Keren has overseen WriteGirl's expansion into a thriving community of women and teen writers and an organization that helps hundreds of Los Angeles girls annually.

Allison Deegan, Ed.D., serves as WriteGirl's Associate Director and has provided critical strategic and operational guidance since the organization's inception in 2001. She participates in all aspects of WriteGirl's leadership, programming and sustainability, and also serves on the WriteGirl Advisory Board. Professionally, Allison is a Business Manager with the Los Angeles County Office of Education, following a career as a marketing and financial consultant. She has made numerous presentations around the country on topics related to after school program success, creative writing and working with youth. She is a mentor, trainer and curriculum consultant with the California School-Age Consortium, which provides professional development to after school program staff. She holds a B.S. in Marketing from Syracuse University, a Master's Degree in Public Policy from California State University, Long Beach, and an Ed.D. in Educational Leadership, also from CSULB. Allison is a screenwriter and fiction writer who has remained close to her WriteGirl mentee, who starts graduate school this fall.

WriteGirl, a creative writing organization for teens, was founded in 2001 in Los Angeles. Through mentoring relationships with professional women writers, workshops, readings and publications, WriteGirl's innovative program offers girls techniques and insights in all genres of writing, helping them to develop communication skills, confidence, self-esteem and an expanded view of themselves and their futures. WriteGirl was awarded a Medal for Service and named the 2010-2011 California Nonprofit of the Year by Governor Arnold Schwarzenegger and First Lady Maria Shriver. In September 2010, WriteGirl received the HUMANITAS Philanthropy Prize, acknowledging WriteGirl's outstanding work of encouraging and empowering writers. WriteGirl is a project of nonprofit organization Community Partners.

OTHER PUBLICATIONS BY WRITEGIRL

Beyond Words: The Creative Voices of WriteGirl

Silhouette: Bold Lines and Voices from WriteGirl

Listen to Me: Shared Secrets from WriteGirl

Lines of Velocity: Words that Move from WriteGirl

Untangled: Stories & Poetry from the Women and Girls of WriteGirl

Nothing Held Back: Truth and Fiction from WriteGirl

Pieces of Me: The Voices of WriteGirl

Bold Ink: Collected Voices of Women & Girls

Threads

Pens on Fire: Creative Writing Experiments for Teens

WriteGirl welcomes your support and involvement: visit WriteGirl
on the web at www.writegirl.org

Don't look back;
forge ahead.
The more you write,
the more you master
the craft.